"There is perhap[s] ... than knowing ho[w] ... [it] out, and move towards a place of trust. Learning such faith in the midst of grief is the topic of this book. Pastorally sensitive and amply rooted in Scripture, it leads us through the 'turning, telling, praying, and trusting' of lament. The author handles the mystery of suffering with care, leading us to Christ, who bore ultimate darkness for us. Some dos and don'ts towards the end of the book represent seasoned wisdom from decades of local church ministry. Questions at the conclusion of chapters not only invite personal reflection but make this a resource that can usefully be read one-to-one or in a small group.

May this book lead many hurting believers into the arms of their loving Father."

Andrew Collins, Certificate Course Director, Biblical Counselling UK, and former consultant psychiatrist

"Paul Mallard writes honestly and movingly from his own personal experiences of profound and inexplicable loss. With gentle wisdom, heartfelt sensitivity, and deep biblical knowledge, he helps us to see the importance of lament in the Christian life. He guides us in how to use biblical words to express our pain and discover afresh the heart of God himself. This is a much-needed book for all those who grieve and those who seek to accompany and support them on their journey."

John Wyatt, emeritus professor of neonatal paediatrics at University College London and author of *Dying Well* and *The Final Lap*

"In *Learning to Lament*, we hear the gentle voice of a pastor sharing truths he himself has learned from the Good Shepherd, our Lord Jesus. Pastorally wise, biblically faithful, and full of helpful illustrations, written in a style accessible to all, this book helps us face up to the unavoidable reality of the many types of painful losses that cause deep grief. Paul Mallard enables believers in our Lord Jesus to see that learning to lament is a necessary part of the normal Christian life: we are encouraged to turn, tell, pray, and trust in the Father of Compassion and the God of all comfort.

This is no sugar-coated discipleship. But as well as addressing the distressing realities of life in a fallen world, Paul helps believers to rest their heads on the pillows of God's sovereignty, goodness, and wisdom. Reading this book alone will nourish your soul, teach you to lament, and help you 'move from "why?" to worship.' Reading the book with others will stimulate honest discussion, Christ-centred encouragement, and mutual support. Having read *Learning to Lament*, I want my friends to read it too!"

Jonathan Prime, Director for Pastoral Support at the Fellowship of Independent Evangelical Churches

"The Christian life is full of joy, but it is also a journey through suffering. *Learning to Lament* gives the reader permission to grieve, to cry out to the Lord in our pain, and to reach out to our brothers and sisters in the church for comfort.

This short book is full of truths that are good for the soul. Read it and find hope. Learn to lament and find comfort in the arms of our good and sovereign Lord."

Keri Folmar, pastor's wife in Dubai, co-host of Priscilla Talk Podcast, author of *The Good Portion: Scripture, How Can Women Thrive in the Local Church?* and *Delighting in the Word Bible Studies*

LEARNING TO LAMENT

OUR HEAVENLY FATHER'S
EMBRACE WHEN WE GRIEVE

Union
Publishing

www.UnionPublishing.org
Bridgend, Wales, United Kingdom

Cover design by somethingmorecreative.com

ISBN (paperback) 978-1-7393426-6-1
ISBN (eBook) 978-1-7393426-7-8

For Edrie, my brave and beautiful girl—
now and forever

ACKNOWLEDGEMENTS

I want to thank all those whose helpful suggestions have shaped this book: Marjie Hutchinson, Hilary and Howard Jackson, and Edrie Mallard.

I also want to thank the congregations at Ladyfield Evangelical Church and Widecombe Baptist Church, Bath. It has been an honour and a privilege to serve you.

CONTENTS

INTRODUCTION: PERMISSION TO LAMENT

Lizzie died when she was thirty-seven.

She was the first member of our immediate family to be snatched away from us.

My wife Edrie's eldest sister had struggled with illness from birth. She'd been born in the 1940s, when hospitals did not yet understand just how devastating maternal deprivation could be. So when she first showed signs of diseased kidneys, she was taken into hospital and isolated from her parents. They could only look through the glass in the window of her ward. Not surprisingly, she didn't recognize them when she eventually returned home.

The shadow of failing kidneys haunted her all her life. But inspired by her faith in Christ, she never surrendered to bitterness or self-pity. I well remember her courage and her wonderful sense of humour. Lizzie refused to let her illness define her—and she had to battle through long years of it.

But in the end, she lost her battle.

Edrie resembled her sister in both looks and personality. The loss of her sister hit her hard.

It was during the months that followed Lizzie's death that I discovered that Christians are not always as sensitive as they should be.

I think of Tony (not his real name), who after church one Sunday came to "comfort" Edrie:

I just want to tell you that I know how you feel. My wife died last year. She is with Jesus. I have never shed a tear for her. Why should I?

And don't let me find you weeping for your sister. Only a selfish person would want her back. So buck up, and don't let the side down.

Yes, he really did say that!

I'd like to tell you that he was the only one. But over the years, I have encountered similar sentiments. "Christians should be stoic" is the underlying narrative. This raises a whole host of questions.

Do we need permission to grieve? Is grief selfish? Should we be afraid of what others think? Are we letting the side down? Is it better to tell lies and pretend we don't feel any grief, saying we are okay when really our lives are falling apart?

So many masks

Christians wear masks. We pretend that all is well when we are actually struggling. Often, the mask we put on is a kind of confident triumphalism which tells the world that our faith is strong and that the trials of this world somehow don't touch us. In particular, we deny the grief and sorrow which we feel in the face of loss.

There are all sorts of reasons we do this.

Perhaps we think that if we confessed our inner struggles, we would be letting the side down. What would my brothers and sisters in church think of me? Their lives are so together and sorted. (If only we knew!) Anyway, there are plenty of people worse off than me. It's better to smile and keep quiet. Isn't that what good Christians do? And what about my witness? What would my non-Christian friends or colleagues think if I told them how I *really* felt?

Then again, we may be suspicious of allowing our feelings to show. Isn't the Christian life a matter of the truth conquering the emotions? We walk by faith, not feelings, distrusting demonstrative displays of strong emotion. We get embarrassed when people open up to us and would never want to inflict our pain on others, for we are terrified of embarrassing or overwhelming them. Surely it's better to be disciplined and controlled?

Then of course there is the whole cacophony of voices around us telling us that triumphant faith conquers everything and we should pull ourselves together. There is no room for pain. Voicing our griefs and sorrows is a denial of God's goodness and a sure sign of unbelief. Remember what happened to Israel in the wilderness? The people grumbled against God and ended up dying outside the promised land.[1] With this in mind, the author of Hebrews warns us, "See to it, brothers and sisters, that none of you has a sinful, unbelieving heart that turns away from the living God" (3:12). Shouldn't we exercise faith instead?

In short, it's better to fix our masks firmly in place and pretend that all is well.

Ditch the mask!

These arguments seem so persuasive—that is, until we turn to the Bible. The root problem here is that we do not know our Bibles well enough. For it is full of men and women who genuinely struggled with pain and loss. And what is so wonderful and unique about the Christian Scriptures is that they tell us the truth about the human condition:

> We know that the whole creation has been groaning as in the pains of childbirth right up to the present time. Not only so, but we ourselves, who have the first-fruits of the Spirit, groan inwardly as we wait eagerly for our adoption to sonship, the redemption of our bodies. (Rom. 8:22–23)

As we shall see, the Bible allows us to be honest. It gives us permission to lament. Lamentation gives grief, sorrow, regret, and disappointment their due. God made us, and he does not expect us to jettison our humanity when we come to faith and are saved. Salvation restores us to what we were always meant

---

1   See Exod. 15:24; 16:2, 7–9, 12; 17:3; Num. 11:1–6; 20:1–3.

to be. And not only is lamenting okay, but it is a vital part of recovering a biblically balanced view of the world.

Lamentation is the prayer language God has given to us so that we can tell him about our sorrows and rekindle our trust in his fatherly care. This was a language used by prophets and apostles, as well as a myriad of unnamed Christians. And this was the language which Jesus himself used in the midst of his trials:

My God, my God, why have you forsaken me?
Why are you so far from saving me,
so far from my cries of anguish? (Ps. 22:1)

And sometimes our own prayers are little more than a groan:

In the same way, the Spirit helps us in our weakness. We do not know what we ought to pray for, but the Spirit himself intercedes for us through wordless groans. (Rom. 8:26)

We know that one day there will be no more tears (Rev. 21:4). But we are not there yet. Today we live between Eden and the new creation, and this place is a vale of tears.

To lament is to be genuinely Christian; sadness does not constitute spiritual failure. We are not "letting the side down" or "spoiling our witness" when we lament. Rather than denying faith, lamentation is an *expression* of faith. As we shall see, we must never confuse a genuine and heartfelt lament or complaint with unbelief and grumbling. As author Mark Vroegop puts it,

"All humans cry; only Christians lament. Lament stands in the gap between pain and promise."[2]

If we are to depend on God in all things, we must learn to mourn, bringing our grief to God, expressing our very real emotions in a healthy way. There are two main Hebrew words translated "lament." One carries the idea of a dirge—a sombre song expressing grief. The other can mean to groan with pain and sorrow. In both cases, the lamenting or mourning is vocal and demonstrative.

When we cry out to God in pain, trusting however feebly in his love, then in pain and lamentation we can be sure of his smile, because "the LORD delights in those who fear him, who put their hope in his unfailing love" (Ps. 147:10–11). As we turn our broken hearts towards God, we discover his kindness and goodness. We feel the warm embrace of our loving heavenly Father. We find boundless comfort in the grace of our precious Saviour. We hear whispers of reassurance as we are drawn into the fellowship of the Holy Spirit. Our broken hearts draw us to delight in the compassionate heart of our triune God.

And this is a precious place to be.

We often mistakenly believe that our strength is what God wants from us, when it is actually brokenness which pleases his heart:

But he said to me, "My grace is sufficient for you, for

---

2   Mark Vroegop, *Dark Clouds, Deep Mercy: Discovering the Grace of Lament* (Wheaton, IL: Crossway 2019), 16.

my power is made perfect in weakness." Therefore I will boast all the more gladly about my weaknesses, so that Christ's power may rest on me. That is why, for Christ's sake, I delight in weaknesses, in insults, in hardships, in persecutions, in difficulties. For when I am weak, then I am strong. (2 Cor. 12:9–10)

So, rather than discouraging healthy expressions of emotion—whether of joy or of pain—the Bible urges us to be honest. It also wants us to recognize that sharing our pain with our Christian family is a good thing. We are in this together, weeping with those who weep (see Rom. 12:15).

We need to learn the language of lamentation.

We need to learn to lament.

1

Understanding and Navigating Grief

The first time I met Edna, she really opened her heart to me.

I had been invited to lead a church house party. The organizers wanted me to speak on the Bible's teaching about marriage. So I took them to God's institution of the covenant of marriage in the garden of Eden, where God defined it in specific and precise terms: "That is why a man leaves his father and mother and is united to his wife, and they become one flesh" (Gen. 2:24).

I developed this further. Marriage is an exclusive, lifelong, covenantal relationship between one man and one woman. No other human relationship is as all-embracing and as all-consuming. And marriage reflects a deeper and even more profound relationship—that between God and Israel (Ezek. 16:8–14; Hos. 2:7), and between Christ and his church (John 3:29; Eph. 5:25–33; Rev. 19:7–9). Sin has disrupted this, but God's purpose in grace is to restore both the vertical and horizontal relationships which, as human beings, we ache for.

Describing love, I outlined where the author of Song of

Solomon says,

Place me like a seal over your heart, like a seal on your arm; for love is as strong as death, its jealousy unyielding as the grave. It burns like blazing fire, like a mighty flame. Many waters cannot quench love; rivers cannot sweep it away. If one were to give all the wealth of one's house for love, it would be utterly scorned. (8:6–7)

Love is as strong as death—and we don't negotiate with death, for it is powerful and uncompromising. It will have its way. And so will love. It blazes like a voracious fire, and everything melts in its heat. That is why the Bible is so insistent that it is only within the covenant of marriage—the lifelong commitment of one man and one woman—that the passions of love can be fully unleashed.

When I had finished, Edna asked to speak with me. She must have been in her seventies, and she spoke with a quiet dignity which made her words even more poignant:

Thank you for what you said, but may I ask you a question? What happens when the man you have loved all your adult life dies? Tom and I were together as far back as I can remember. Sometimes I forget that he is gone and shout out his name. I don't want to live without Tom. I know it's wrong, but I can't help it. If it is true that love is a fire that burns, then I am being consumed by the flames.

Powerful words. And I didn't know what to say.

Writing about the death of his wife Joy, whom he'd married later in life, the don and writer C. S. Lewis used a medical analogy to describe his excruciating experience:

> To say the patient is getting over it after an operation for appendicitis is one thing; after he's had his leg off it is quite another. After that operation either the wounded stump heals or the man dies. If it heals, the fierce, continuous pain will stop. Presently he'll get back his strength and be able to stump about on his wooden leg. He has "got over it." But he will probably have recurrent pains in the stump all his life, and perhaps pretty bad ones; and he will always be a one-legged man.[1]

Sometimes the amputee will get out of bed in the middle of the night and fall flat on his face because he's forgotten for a moment that he has lost a limb. Even with the best prosthesis in the world, he may limp for the rest of his life.

And Edna will limp until she gets to heaven.

Psychiatrist Elisabeth Kübler-Ross and counsellor David Kessler put it like this:

> The reality is that you will grieve forever. You will not "get over" the loss of a loved one; you will learn to live with it. You will heal and you will rebuild yourself around the loss

---

1   C. S. Lewis, *A Grief Observed* (London: Faber & Faber, 2015), 52.

you have suffered. You will be whole again but you will never be the same. Nor should you be the same, nor would you want to.[2]

In our particular experience of brokenness, we also need to learn to limp.

The experience of grief

Grief is the universal, unavoidable, and harrowing reaction to loss. Later, we will explore grief and lamentation in the broadest possible terms. That loss can be physical (e.g., disability or dementia), social (e.g., divorce or childlessness), economic (e.g., bankruptcy), occupational (e.g., redundancy) or spiritual (e.g., feeling abandoned by God). However, our initial focus will be on the grief which engulfs us when we lose a person close to us.

Those who have experienced loss are sometimes called "bereaved." The word "bereave" comes from an Old English word meaning "to deprive of, to take away by violence, to seize or to rob." Some deaths are comparatively peaceful, but the experience of bereavement may feel like an act of violence. Someone we embraced has been ripped from our arms. We may feel plundered, violated even.

So, how do we react to such a brutal experience? There is, of course, no standard reaction—grief can take many forms. It may well include denial, anger, guilt, anxiety, fear, and despair.

---

2   Elisabeth Kübler-Ross and David Kessler, *On Grief & Grieving: Finding the Meaning of Grief Through the Five Stages of Loss* (New York: Simon & Schuster, 2014), 230.

Sometimes it manifests itself in physical symptoms: we cannot sleep; we have no appetite; we lose interest in everything. As Christians we might feel that God has abandoned us: how could he be so cruel?

All these things are normal. In and of itself, grief is neither a pathological condition nor a personality disorder. And Christians are not immune.

We may try to avoid pain by bottling up our emotions—avoiding those places and items which remind us of our loved one. But tiny things will set us off. My dad wore aftershave from a little bottle with a ship on the side. For months after his death, even its faintest aroma would bring tears to my eyes.

The journey through the wilderness of grief is both harsh and harrowing, so we may want to move through it very quickly. But we have to learn patience in our pain, and the only way to move through this unwelcome territory is just that: to move through it. Failing to grieve means storing up trouble for the future. Physical healing involves convalescence and perseverance, and the same is true of the damage done by grief. We have to work through the process before we can leave the wilderness. And beware! It may take longer than you expect.

We've noted already that the Bible gives us permission to grieve. Listen to what David says on the death of his son:

The king was shaken. He went up to the room over the gateway and wept. As he went, he said: "O my son Absalom! My son, my son Absalom! If only I had died instead of you—O Absalom, my son, my son!" (2 Sam. 18:33)

Here is the grief of a father—a poignant mixture of anguish and guilt and heartbreak.

We are to remember:

> The LORD is near to those who have a broken heart and saves such as have a contrite spirit. (Ps. 34:18)

And Jesus invites us to come to him with our tears: "Come to Me, all you who labor and are heavy laden, and I will give you rest" (Matt. 11:28 NKJV). He promises, "Blessed are those who mourn, for they shall be comforted" (Matt. 5:4 NKJV).

Why we grieve

Grief is inescapable because we are human beings. God has set eternity in our hearts (Eccl. 5:11), and we know deep down that death is an aberration; we cannot rationalize it. It disturbs and shatters us and shakes us to the core of our beings. It just feels so wrong—not like the ways things were meant to be. Indeed, the story of the Bible tells us that death was not part of the original creation.

When we become Christians, we do not shed our humanity. To be human is to experience brokenness, frailty, and frustration—our Christian faith does not lift us above these things. Moreover, sadness does not constitute spiritual failure. The creation groans, and so do we:

> We know that the whole creation has been groaning as in the pains of childbirth right up to the present time. Not

only so, but we ourselves, who have the firstfruits of the
Spirit, groan inwardly as we wait eagerly for our adoption
to sonship, the redemption of our bodies. (Rom. 8:22–23)

Labour pains are intense but productive. Indeed, pain is the
portal to life. But we should not deny either the intensity of
the pain or the reality of the hope. When we grieve, we are not
"letting the side down" or "spoiling our witness." We need to be
honest about how we feel and seek a more wholesome biblical
answer to our grief, rather than trying to pretend that it is not
real.

Grief isn't something that we should hope to avoid—or some-
thing that happens to only a few. Grief touches all of us—great
and small. Who can forget the devastating photograph of Queen
Elizabeth II at the funeral of her husband? She sat alone, because
Prince Philip had died during lockdown at the height of the
COVID-19 restrictions. The photo eloquently captures her grief.
One commentator quoted her words, spoken just after 9/11:
"Grief is the price we pay for love."

And that is the point. Love is painful. We will focus later
on how it cost God his only beloved Son to redeem our fallen
and rebellious world. It cost the Son the eternal sunshine of the
Father's smile as he took our place on the cross. It is impossible
to know what happened during those hours of darkness. Christ,
who was sinless, experienced the wrath of his Father on behalf
of all his people. The wonderful eternal unity of Father, Son, and
Holy Spirit could never be disrupted. Yet the Son experienced a

sense of lostness that defies explanation.[3] Love is painful. When we love, we find our lives entwined.

On our fortieth wedding anniversary, one of the cards which Edrie and I received included a picture of two trees. They had grown side by side and over the years had become entwined. The greeting said, "You belong together!"

Imagine what would happen if you tried to remove one of those trees. Could you do it without badly damaging the other one? Probably not. But that is what bereavement does. It involves fracture and tearing apart and dislocation. The more we love, the more we grieve.

Listen to Nicholas Wolterstorff as he laments the death of his twenty-five-year-old son Eric, who died in a mountain-climbing accident:

> But we all suffer. For we all prize and love; and in this present existence of ours, prizing and loving yield suffering. Love in our world is suffering love. Suffering is for the loving. In commanding us to love, God invites us to suffer.[4]

Enemy or friend?

For those who do not know Christ, death can only ever be an enemy. It is the grave of hope. But for believers, the relationship is ambivalent.

On the one hand, death was the result of the fall (Gen. 2:17),

---

3   See John 2:16; Rom. 5:6–8; 1 John 3:16; 4:10.

4   Nicholas Wolterstorff, *Lament for a Son* (Grand Rapids: Eerdmans, 1987), 89.

and it will be the last enemy to be defeated (1 Cor. 15:25–26; Rev. 21:4). But we are part of this flesh-and-blood world, and we want to continue to glorify God and enjoy him here and now. God wants us to receive his gifts with gratitude and to savor them:

Every good and perfect gift is from above, coming down from the Father of the heavenly lights, who does not change like shifting shadows. (James 1:17)

It would be churlish indeed to reject such gifts: a good meal with friends, a much-needed holiday, a task satisfyingly completed. We should be engaged in this world as fully as Jesus was, and we should not be in any hurry to leave.

On the other hand, death means to depart and be with Jesus. It is the passage from a prison into a palace. If we forget our ultimate destination, we may become so absorbed with the gifts that we forget the Giver. Nothing in this world is perfect—no pleasure, no relationship, no ambition can ever satisfy our hearts, for we were made to find our satisfaction in the triune God. As believers, we begin to experience eternal life now, and therefore we long for its completion beyond the veil of death.

So is our deepest longing to stay or to go? This dilemma puts Paul in a quandary. He writes from prison to his friends in Philippi:

If I am to go on living in the body, this will mean fruitful labor for me. Yet what shall I choose? I do not know! I am torn between the two: I desire to depart and be with

Christ, which is better by far; but it is more necessary for you that I remain in the body. (Phil. 1:22–24)

This ambivalence affects both the way we think of death and the way in which we grieve. So how do we comfort those who grieve?

Paul comforts grieving Christians in this way:

Brothers and sisters, we do not want you to be uninformed about those who sleep in death, so that you do not grieve like the rest of mankind, who have no hope. For we believe that Jesus died and rose again, and so we believe that God will bring with Jesus those who have fallen asleep in him. (1 Thess. 4:14–15)

This passage, which we will return to later, brims with Christian hope. Those who have died in Christ are now experiencing rest from trouble in the sleep of death.[5] Grieving people need compassion, and they need truth and hope. And there is plenty of hope here, for our grief is not hopeless like that of those who are not in Christ. But notice that Paul does not forbid grieving. In fact, the clear implication is that they (and by implication we) are to grieve. But in a Christian way.

This is where we have to be careful. As we minister hope, we must never be mealy-mouthed about the "blessings of death" or

---

5   This is not "soul-sleep," as we shall see later. Rather, Paul is speaking of the rest which the soul experiences after the death of the body.

otherwise insensitive to those who grieve. Think of the man who wakes in the morning and reaches across to the warm part of the bed where his wife has lain with him for over forty years. In that moment between sleep and consciousness, he forgets that she is gone. He reaches across, but the bed is cold.

Don't tell him, "She is with the Lord—it's selfish to grieve!" We can believe in the resurrection but still have broken hearts and weep scalding tears. Jesus did. He knew that he had the power to raise the dead (John 11:25–26), but this did not stop him from grieving at Lazarus' tomb (vv. 33–35). There Jesus was moved with intense sorrow at the vileness of death and at the grief of his friends. (We shall also return to this later.)

The zigzag of grief

Nothing can prepare us for the death of a loved one and the excruciating pain that follows. Each experience of grief is unique, for grieving is a personal journey, and there is no right way to grieve. Grief is also a "process," because it involves moving through a serious of emotions. In their book *On Grief & Grieving*, Kübler-Ross and Kessler identify five stages of grief: denial, anger, bargaining, depression, and acceptance. This is helpful to know, but we should avoid being too prescriptive or rigid, for grief is not linear, but more like a zigzag line moving back and forth from devastating pain to unexpected relief.

So how do we respond?

We will need to be patient—we cannot rush the grieving process. Often things will get worse before they get better. We want to jump straight to the insight that God meant it for good (Gen.

50:20), but God operates on his own timescale, and we cannot hold an hourglass to the Creator of time.

At the same time, we need to remind ourselves that every sorrow has its limits: "Weeping may last for a night, but joy comes in the morning" (Ps. 30:5). No night lasts forever. The sun will rise, and dawn will come. As a victim of a concentration camp expressed it:

> I believe in the sun even when it is not shining.
> I believe in love
> where feeling is not.
> I believe in God even if he is silent.[6]

When we lose someone we love, our challenge is to accept the reality of our loss and adjust to a new environment. This will involve being honest, vulnerable, and open about our heartbreak, confusion, and despair. It will often bring uncertainty, pain, and a questioning of faith. But if I fail to acknowledge those realities, then I am locking myself into a world where sorrow, pain, heartbreak, and loss will *only* be negative things. By naming my feelings, and by being honest about them, I can enter into them more fully and can find a way of dealing with them.

It may be a shocking thing to say, but we can glorify God through our grief. As God's people, we are called to glorify him in all circumstances (1 Cor. 6:20; 10:31). And this must include

---

6   Anonymous words written on the wall of a cellar in a concentration camp in Cologne by a Jewish victim of Nazi persecution in the Second World War. They are the concluding words of Terry Waite's autobiography, *Taken on Trust* (London: Coronet, 1994), 447.

the way we deal with loss, strange though that may seem. But obviously, this does not mean that we jettison our emotions and sublimate our grief. We don't glorify God in grief by forcing a smile.

And this is where lamenting comes in.

Lamenting faithfully

Job is someone from whom we can learn in this context. He glorified God even in the grief of multiple bereavements, and not once did he charge God with evil:

> At this, Job got up and tore his robe and shaved his
> head. Then he fell to the ground in worship and said:
>> "Naked I came from my mother's womb,
>> and naked I will depart.
>> The LORD gave and the LORD has taken away;
>> may the name of the LORD be praised."
> In all this, Job did not sin by charging God with
> wrongdoing. (Job 1:20–22)

And yet Job did lament his losses. We need to help our friends to lament. Often we want to say something positive. But even as we do so, we may sense the banality of our words. If only we were familiar with the gift of lament, we could be more helpful. Listen to Job again:

> May the day of my birth perish,
> and the night that said, "A boy is conceived!" (3:3)

Why did I not perish at birth,
    and die as I came from the womb? (3:11)

Why is light given to those in misery,
    and life to the bitter of soul,
to those who long for death that does not come,
    who search for it more than for hidden treasure,
who are filled with gladness
    and rejoice when they reach the grave? (3:20–22)

This is exceedingly painful to read: there is nothing polite or composed or detached about Job's words. Here is the language of lament, the vocabulary of complaint: Why did God bless me with life only to shatter it? Although Job is addressing his so-called counsellors, he knows, as do we, that his words are really directed to the God whom he has been devoted to (1:1, 8; 2:3). How can God appear to be acting so out of character?

As a pastor, I've heard this so many times:

Why did you give me a husband to walk with and then snatch him away? … How can I ever be the same again? You put a daughter into my arms, and she was such a delight. How can a little life, so small, leave a gap in my heart a million miles wide? … O God, I know you love me, but right now you seem so cruel.

This may be the scream of the soul, but it is also part of the healing process. You can be honest with God!

Sometimes we short-circuit the grieving, and therefore the

healing, process. In an attempt to bring comfort to the bereaved, we turn a funeral into a thanksgiving service. The motive is good, and the outcome often beneficial. But do we leave time for genuine sorrow and grief?

There is all the difference in the world between the funeral of a Christian and that of someone with no faith—it's true. But are we sometimes so concerned to express that difference that we leave no room for genuine expressions of anguish, like the scalding tears of grief? Giving ourselves and others permission to grieve does not negate our gratefulness or deny God's goodness. A Christian funeral should express *both* triumphant hope and honest heartbreak.

When we lament, we are talking to God, turning to him in pain and telling him all our heart's anguish. This in itself is an act of faith, for lament involves setting our complaints before God. Yet we often see lament as an act of unbelief. In reality, it is the exact opposite. Beneath our cries lies confusion about the disparity between conviction and experience—how can the God I know and love act like this? But as we turn our complaints into prayers, we open ourselves up to God's grace and can trust his promises afresh.

Love hurts

One of the first books I read as a young Christian was *Through Gates of Splendour.*[7] The author, Elisabeth Elliot, had been born

---

7   Elisabeth Elliot, *Through Gates of Splendour,* 3rd ed. (Bletchley, UK: Authentic Media, 2005).

to missionary parents and had served as a missionary in Ecuador. In 1953 she married Jim Elliot, and together they began translating the New Testament into the language of the Quechua Indians. Ten months later, Jim, along with four other missionaries, was killed by the Auca Indians while attempting to take the gospel to this unreached tribe. In spite of her heartbreak, Elisabeth went on to live and work among the Aucas.

The title of her book is taken from the words of a well-known hymn which speaks of the challenge of following Christ, even into death:

We rest on Thee, our Shield and our Defender;
Thine is the battle; Thine shall be the praise,
When passing through the gates of pearly splendour,
Victors, we rest with Thee, through endless days.[8]

The story demonstrates enormous courage and faith. But Elisabeth still found that the loss of her husband shook her to the very core. Writing many years later, she admits,

When I stood by my shortwave radio in the jungle of Ecuador in 1956 and heard that my husband, Jim Elliot, was missing, God brought to my mind the words of the prophet Isaiah: "When thou passest through the waters, I will be with thee" (Isa. 43:2). You can imagine that my response was not terribly spiritual. I was saying, "But Lord,

---

8 Edith G. Cherry, "We Rest on Thee, Our Shield and Our Defender," 1895.

you're with me all the time. What I want is *Jim*. I want my husband." We had been married 27 months after waiting five-and-a-half years.

Five days later I knew that Jim was dead. And God's presence with me was not Jim's presence. That was a terrible fact. God's presence didn't change the terrible fact that I was a widow, and I expected to be a widow until I died because I thought it was a miracle I got married the first time.

Here is honest, raw lament.

We can only imagine the questions that flooded Elisabeth's mind:

It's not fair! Where are you God? Why give me a husband and then take him away so soon? Why take him when he was only seeking to serve you?

But she does not end there:

Jim's absence thrust me, forced me, hurried me to God, my hope and my only refuge.

And I learned in that experience who God is in a way I could never have known otherwise. And so I can say to you that suffering is an irreplaceable medium through which I learned an indispensable truth: God is God.[9]

---

9   From Elisabeth Elliot, *Suffering Is Never for Nothing* (Nashville: B&H Books, 2019), as

When we lament, we turn to God and pour out our complaints before him. But we do not stop there. Lamentation brings us to see him more clearly and discover that "God is God." Biblical lamenting never leads us to a dead end. It always leads us to God.

Questions

1. "You will heal and you will rebuild yourself around the loss you have suffered. You will be whole again but you will never be the same. Nor should you be the same nor would you want to."[10] Is this true in your experience? Explain your answer.

2. The Father bore the loss of his Son, and the Son bore the loss of his Father, in order to save his enemies. How does this truth help us when we grieve?

3. Augustine, the great church father, was almost overwhelmed by raw grief when his mother died. But when he allowed his emotions to express themselves in a flood of tears, he found relief: "The tears streamed down, and I let them flow as freely as they would, making them a pillow for my heart. On them I rested."[11] Why do you think God gave us tear ducts? How do we find rest through tears?

4. "We do not want you to be uninformed about those who sleep in death, so that you do not grieve like the rest of mankind, who have no hope" (1 Thess. 4:13). How is our grief the same as that of those who have no hope? And how is it

adapted by the editors of The Gospel Coalition, February 18, 2019.

10 Kübler-Ross and Kessler, *On Grief & Grieving*, 230.

11 Augustine, *Confessions*, IX.33.

different?

5. "And so I can say to you that suffering is an irreplaceable medium through which I learned an indispensable truth: God is God,"[12] said Elisabeth Elliot. How can grief cause us to see that "God is God"?

---

12 Elliot, *Suffering*, 2019, as adapted by The Gospel Coalition, February 18, 2019.

2

Learning to Be Honest about
Loss and Suffering

Life is about losing things.

And losing things can be incredibly painful.

So far, we have focused on the loss of people we love, and we have noted that faith and hope do not remove the anguish and pain of bereavement. Grief is the universal, unavoidable, and harrowing reaction to loss. So while Christians do not grieve like people who have no hope, they do still grieve.

This sense of grief can accompany a wide variety of losses. It can be physical. I have a grandson who was born with the most severe, life-limiting disabilities. As I hold little Abraham in my arms, I lament the fact that he will never reach the potential for which we hope with the birth of every child. Or I think of my mum in her last years, when dementia had robbed her of almost all personality; she had become a ghost at our table.

Or the loss may be social. Marriage is supposed to be permanent, and most people enter it intending to make a life-long commitment. But sometimes it is painful: "After being patient for so long, why is my marriage so miserable?" Or the marriage may be marked by infidelity: "How can I trust anyone again when I feel so betrayed?" Perhaps the marriage is happy, but the longing for family life is not fulfilled: "I can't go to church on Mother's Day since we learned that we won't be able to have children."

The loss may be economic or occupational. We often define ourselves by our work or our wealth, and this may be unwise. But the Bible does see work as a God-given gift, and we know that it teaches us not to despise the good things God gives us. So, redundancy or long-term unemployment may be a cause for genuine grief. I have met many who struggle to come to terms with retirement and a loss of status. A loss of financial security can also bring with it an acute sense of mourning.

Beyond this, Christians may experience grief because of spiritual loss. How do I cope when God seems so far away and heaven is silent? How do I handle it when someone I love turns away from the faith? How do I respond when the church which I love falls apart or becomes toxic? What do I do when the Christian values on which my whole culture has built its foundations disappear around me—"gone with the wind"?

We could go on. Whenever we lose something we cherish, we can be engulfed by grief, as in a bereavement.

Folded into the fabric

Loss and suffering are folded into the very fabric of our lives.

The only condition for experiencing suffering is to live long enough. Sometimes suffering seems unjust and disproportionate. It may be the cost of faithfully following a crucified Saviour, or it may simply be that of being human.

Eliphaz reminded Job, "Yet man is born to trouble as surely as sparks fly upward" (Job 5:7). Job agreed, saying, "Mortals, born of woman, are of few days and full of trouble" (14:1).

Gazing at thousands of graves in the wilderness, Moses laments,

> You turn people back to dust,
>   saying, "Return to dust, you mortals."
> A thousand years in your sight
>   are like a day that has just gone by,
>   or like a watch in the night.
> Yet you sweep people away in the sleep of death—
>   they are like the new grass of the morning:
> In the morning it springs up new,
>   but by evening it is dry and withered. (Ps. 90:3–6)

Paul reminds the Corinthians that we have a great treasure in the gospel, but he clarifies that

> we have this treasure in jars of clay to show that this all-surpassing power is from God and not from us. We are hard pressed on every side, but not crushed; perplexed, but not in despair; persecuted, but not abandoned; struck down, but not destroyed. We always carry around in our body the death of Jesus, so that the life of Jesus may also be revealed in our body. (2 Cor. 4:7–10)

Pastor and author Tim Keller captures this well when he writes,

> No matter what precautions we take, no matter how well we have put together a good life, no matter how hard we have worked to be healthy, wealthy, comfortable with friends and family, and successful with our career—something will inevitably ruin it.[1]

Loss and suffering are arguably the greatest ongoing challenges to the Christian faith. They are more than philosophical issues—they affect us at the deepest possible level. We long for an explanation which will somehow give meaning to our pain, or even to others', but all too often, it is elusive.

There is a grand Bible narrative which explains why we suffer. In the beginning, there was no pain or suffering in Eden, but our sin means that we are no longer in that garden. The creation groans, and so do we (Rom. 8:22–23). Through Christ, the new age has dawned, but we are still waiting for its consummation. In new resurrection bodies, we will one day experience perfect physical, mental, and relational health for all eternity. Then we will enjoy a restored and perfected garden (Rev. 22:1–5).

This is a wonderful story—the greatest story ever. And it is true. But when we suffer, its truth can seem so theoretical and distant. Loss becomes such a reality that our ears may be stopped

---

1   Timothy Keller, *Walking with God through Pain and Suffering* (New York: Penguin, 2013), 3.

to the genuine comfort that this story brings. There seems to be such a disparity between expectation and experience, between hope and outcome.

Loss of hope can rip us apart: "Hope deferred makes the heart sick, but a longing fulfilled is a tree of life" (Prov. 13:12).

The pain that follows may be a passing emotion for a temporary loss, or it can strike at the very core of our lives and permanently hang over us like a shadow: "Always winter but never Christmas."[2]

A cacophony of unhelpful voices

Here's an insight which I received as a young pastor from a much more experienced minister:

What you need to remember is that Christians tell lies. They do it with good motives, but they do it nonetheless. It happens around midday on a Sunday at the back of the church. You are shaking hands at the door, and as they leave, you ask them how they are doing. They look you in the eye and tell you that they are doing fine. But you know the reality: that their lives are falling apart.

We have already seen how Christians often deny the depths of their emotions. We hide our doubts and fears because we think they reveal a lack of faith.

2   C. S. Lewis, *The Lion, the Witch, and the Wardrobe* (New York: HarperCollins Children's Books, 2009), 19.

We are surrounded by a cacophony of unhelpful voices which clamour to be heard—the voices of the ones my friend describes as the "blessed band of helpful healers." They assure us that as Christians, we have the right to be healed. Just a little more faith will enable us to receive our "healing." This "healing" may be physical, emotional, or financial, but in any case, it is ours by right. So we should give no room to any negative thoughts.

The pain of loss makes us vulnerable, so we may listen to such seductive voices. But they are wrong. And at so many levels. Yes, we hope for total healing and restoration when we get to heaven, but we are not there yet. Pain was Jesus' pathway—from the cross to the crown, as we will see later—and we follow in his wake. The only people who tell you that they have an instant route to health, wealth, and happiness are likely trying to sell you something. *Caveat emptor!*[3]

Then there is the harsh voice of Christian stoicism. It takes the pain seriously, but it baulks at the emotions which pain provokes. It tells us:

Submit to God's purposes … Loss is good because it helps you cut your ties to the people and places and pleasures of this world … Stifle your tears … Pull yourself together … Don't let the side down … Think about heaven.

But this voice is dead to the constant refrain in Scripture. The best of God's people lament, and they are not reprimanded for it.

---

3   "Let the buyer beware!"

So, this voice may be "stoic," but it is not Christian.

Finally, there is the voice of indulgent self-pity. Suffering has a way of turning us in on ourselves. And it is easy to become imprisoned in negative emotions: anger, bitterness, frustration, helplessness, fear, and guilt. We descend into a maelstrom from which we cannot escape. Paul reminds the Ephesians,

Do not let any unwholesome talk come out of your mouths, but only what is helpful for building others up according to their needs, that it may benefit those who listen. And do not grieve the Holy Spirit of God, with whom you were sealed for the day of redemption. Get rid of all bitterness, rage and anger, brawling and slander, along with every form of malice. (Eph. 4:29–31)

Here Paul is thinking about relationships rather than suffering. But the cocktail of toxic emotions which he describes can be associated with an unhealthy response to grief and loss. Emotions, even in grief, can be healthy and holy. But conversely, they can also become sinful and harmful, and "grieve" the Holy Spirit. This is a love word, a relational word, that reminds us that the Spirit is a person, not an impersonal power. The Spirit comforts us in our grief, but indulgence in sinful emotions frustrates his ministry.

So, how do we get it right? What voice should we listen to? The answer, as always, is the voice of God in Scripture.

Telling and showing

The Bible encourages us to express our grief, whatever our loss, and sometimes it does so in an interesting way. It tells us to cast our cares on the Lord because he cares for us (1 Pet. 5:7). Anxiety is to be met with prayer: "Do not be anxious about anything, but in every situation, by prayer and petition, with thanksgiving, present your requests to God" (Phil. 4:6).

Paul is encouraging us to turn our worry list into our prayer list. This is clearly an invitation to honesty. Behind it lies the invitation of Jesus himself: "Come to me, all you who are weary and burdened, and I will give you rest" (Matt. 11:28).

But beyond this, the Bible shows us a multiplicity of examples of godly people pouring out their woes to God: many of his great servants are honest and authentic about their suffering and confusion.

Moses cries out to God because of the overwhelming burden he feels as he tries to lead forward a rebellious and ungrateful people:

Why have you brought this trouble on your servant? What have I done to displease you that you put the burden of all these people on me? Did I conceive all these people? Did I give them birth? Why do you tell me to carry them in my arms, as a nurse carries an infant, to the land you promised on oath to their ancestors? Where can I get meat for all these people? They keep wailing to me, "Give us meat to eat!" I cannot carry all these people by myself; the burden is too heavy for me. If this is how you are going to treat me, please go ahead and kill me—if I have found favor in your eyes—and do not let me face my own ruin. (Num. 11:11–15)

Elijah laments the apparent failure of God to turn back the tide of evil which he sees all around him:

I have been very zealous for the LORD God Almighty. The Israelites have rejected your covenant, torn down your altars, and put your prophets to death with the sword. I am the only one left, and now they are trying to kill me too. (1 Kings 19:10)

The prophet is sometimes castigated for his lack of courage or the failure of his faith. But personally, I think this is unfair. It is his zeal for God's glory that breaks his heart.

Or think of the honesty of the apostle Paul:

We do not want you to be uninformed, brothers and sisters, about the troubles we experienced in the province of Asia. We were under great pressure, far beyond our ability to endure, so that we despaired of life itself. Indeed, we felt we had received the sentence of death. (2 Cor. 1:8–9)

Later in the same letter he will describe his own anguished cry to God to remove the "thorn" which he felt was blighting his ministry (12:7). Passionately and persistently, he cried: "Three times I pleaded with the Lord to take it away from me" (12:8).

Confessions are good for the soul

Jeremiah preached at a precarious period in the history of God's people, when the nation was on the brink of catastrophic judgement. The prophet lived through the destruction of Jerusalem as it was crushed by the all-powerful Babylonian Empire in 587 BC (2 Kings 25). So, the people lost their temple, their king, and their land. Jeremiah not only saw disaster coming, but he also felt it. He identified with the afflictions of God's people and lamented the fact that they had rejected his message and would not turn back from the precipice. His heartbreak is recorded in "confessions": "The Confessions of Jeremiah," a collection of six first-person poems in the book of Jeremiah.[4]

Like all godly laments, these confessions flow from Jeremiah's communion with God. They express an inner conflict of soul. Here is a sensitive man who sees more clearly than anyone else and yet is rejected and mocked and physically attacked. Like Cassandra, he tells the truth, but no one believes him.[5]

Jeremiah feels as if he cannot hold on—the task God has given him is crushing. If he didn't care, it would be bearable, but he is passionate for God's reputation and glory, and so he is devastated. The task is too much for him, and in words that border on the intemperate, he cries out to God,

You deceived me, LORD, and I was deceived;
   you overpowered me and prevailed.

---

4   See Jeremiah 11:18–23; 12:1–6; 15:10–21; 17:14–18; 18:19–23; 20:7–13.

5   In Homer's *Iliad*, Cassandra was a Trojan priestess who prophesied the fall of Troy but was not believed.

I am ridiculed all day long;
  everyone mocks me.
Whenever I speak, I cry out
  proclaiming violence and destruction.
So the word of the LORD has brought me
  insult and reproach all day long. (Jer. 20:7–8)

In spite of this opposition, he has to go on preaching:

But if I say, "I will not mention his word
  or speak anymore in his name,"
his word is in my heart like a fire,
  a fire shut up in my bones.
I am weary of holding it in;
  indeed, I cannot. (v. 9)

There is a clash between Jeremiah's divine calling and the reception of his message. He feels trapped, and in words reminiscent of Job, he rues the day of his birth:

Cursed be the day I was born!
  May the day my mother bore me not be blessed!
Cursed be the man who brought my father the news,
  who made him very glad, saying,
  "A child is born to you—a son!"
May that man be like the towns
  the LORD overthrew without pity.
May he hear wailing in the morning,

a battle cry at noon.
For he did not kill me in the womb,
  with my mother as my grave,
  her womb enlarged forever.
Why did I ever come out of the womb
  to see trouble and sorrow
  and to end my days in shame? (vv. 14–18)

Jeremiah's life is smothered by a suffocating melancholy. Ministry is not supposed to be like this! Here is a faithful servant of God being honest about the nearly impossible task which God has given him. How will he cope when disaster strikes?

Lamenting with Jeremiah

And of course the worst does happen. The sword falls, and Judah is taken into exile:

After affliction and harsh labor,
  Judah has gone into exile.
She dwells among the nations;
  she finds no resting place.
All who pursue her have overtaken her
  in the midst of her distress. (Lam. 1:3)

It is in this context that the prophet writes the five laments that make up the book of Lamentations. Jeremiah does not distance himself from God's people, even though they have rejected his words. There is no "told-you-so" self-righteousness here:

My eyes fail from weeping,
   I am in torment within;
my heart is poured out on the ground
   because my people are destroyed,
because children and infants faint
   in the streets of the city. (2:11)

Repentance and a return to God are demanded. The book is a "complete cleansing of the conscience through a total confession of sin":[6]

Let us examine our ways and test them,
   and let us return to the Lord.
Let us lift up our hearts and our hands
   to God in heaven, and say:
"We have sinned and rebelled
   and you have not forgiven." (3:40–42)

The nation knows that she is being crushed in the winepress of God's wrath:

The Lord has rejected
   all the warriors in my midst;
he has summoned an army against me
   to crush my young men.
In his winepress the Lord has trampled

6   Norman Gottwald, *Studies in the Book of Lamentations* (London: SCM Press, 1954), 30.

Virgin Daughter Judah. (1:15)

Yahweh is behind the suffering of God's people—it is not arbitrary or unjust. "No accident, no demon, no foreign god was responsible for the plight of Israel, but Yahweh alone," according to Norman Gottwald.[7]

But crucially, lamentation and hope are not mutually exclusive. Sprinkled through Lamentations are short prayers crying to God for aid. The whole of chapter 5 is a prayer, and the book itself ends on an appeal for mercy:

Restore us to yourself, Lord, that we may return;
    renew our days as of old
unless you have utterly rejected us
    and are angry with us beyond measure. (5:21–22)

The third poem is the heart of the book, and the heart of this poem is the confession of God's covenant faithfulness (see Exod. 34:6–7):

Because of the Lord's great love, we are not consumed,
    for his compassions never fail.
They are new every morning;
    great is your faithfulness.
I say to myself, "The Lord is my portion;
    therefore I will wait for him."

---

7   Gottwald, *Lamentations*, 77.

The LORD is good to those whose hope is in him,
    to the one who seeks him;
it is good to wait quietly
    for the salvation of the LORD.
It is good for a man to bear the yoke
    while he is young. (3:22–27)

When we put together the confessions and the lamentations of Jeremiah, we see the brutal honesty of one of God's choicest servants. But before we condemn this honesty, remember that he is talking to the God who already knows his heart. Jeremiah's struggles help us today as we too struggle. The prophets were not supermen striding above the painful battles of life, but were as human and as fragile as we are. We too are allowed to have doubts and fears and perplexities, and to tell the God who already knows our hearts. The redeeming factor is that Jeremiah knew that he could turn to God in his perplexity. Perhaps he would have shared Peter's sentiment: "Lord, to whom shall we go? You have the words of eternal life" (John 6:68).

Jeremiah, the "weeping prophet," is a type of Christ, who would also warn of judgement (Luke 19:41–44) and weep over Jerusalem (Matt. 23:37). He points to Christ as the One who shares our suffering and pain and fragile humanity. In Christ we have a greater model than Jeremiah. Are we allowed to be honest about our perplexities and struggles? Yes, we certainly are, for our Saviour leads the way.

But what form should our laments take?

For the answer, we will next turn to the book of Psalms.

Questions

1. "Losing things is incredibly painful." Why does loss hurt so much? This is very sensitive territory, but what has been your most painful experience of loss?

2. Suffering is arguably the greatest challenge to the Christian faith. Why do you think this is the case? How does honesty help?

3. "The only people who tell you that they have an instant route to health, wealth, and happiness are likely trying to sell you something!" Why shouldn't we buy what they are selling?

4. Why is the voice of Christian stoicism attractive? And why is it wrong?

5. Read the confessions of Jeremiah (Jer. 11:18–23; 12:1–6, 15:10–21; 17:14–18; 18:19–23; 20:7–13.) What was troubling Jeremiah here? What did he do about it?

3

Learning the Language of Lament

Lamenting is vital. Indeed, it is dangerous not to lament.

As Mark Vroegop puts it,

Lament is how we bring our sorrow to God. Without lament we won't know how to process pain. Silence, bitterness, and even anger can dominate our spiritual lives instead. Without lament we won't know how to help people walking through sorrow. Instead, we'll offer trite solutions, unhelpful comments, or impatient responses. What's more, without this sacred song of sorrow, we'll miss the lessons historic laments are intended to teach us.

Lament is how Christians grieve. It is how to help hurting people. Lament is how we learn important truths about God and our world."[1]

1   Vroegop, *Dark Clouds, Deep Mercy*, 21.

We've already noted the golden seam of lamentation running through the Bible. The very fact that this is recorded in Scripture should challenge any reticence we might have about being honest with God. We must learn to mourn and bring our grief to him, expressing our emotions in a healthy way.

Failure to lament is dangerous for our emotional and spiritual wellbeing and may lead to toxic emotions such as bitterness, envy, and self-pity. In some cases these emotions may fuel unbelief. And just as it is crucial to our physical health for a septic wound to be drained, so too it is vital to our mental and spiritual health for us to express our emotions in a wholesome and healthy way.

When suppressed, grief may lead to ungodly anger. It is right to be angry with death and its impact on our lives—Jesus himself was. But it can never be healthy to be angry with God. Job got near to this, but later he repented:

> Then Job replied to the LORD,
> "I know that you can do all things;
>   no purpose of yours can be thwarted.
> You asked, 'Who is this that obscures my plans
>   without knowledge?'
> Surely I spoke of things I did not understand,
>   things too wonderful for me to know.
>
> "You said, 'Listen now, and I will speak;
>   I will question you,
>   and you shall answer me.'
> My ears had heard of you

but now my eyes have seen you.
Therefore I despise myself
   and repent in dust and ashes." (Job 42:1–6)

Ungodly anger may bear ugly fruit.

We might experience bitterness and envy. We can easily feel that we do not deserve this—why are others happy when I have lost the person or the thing that I love?

But perhaps the most dangerous manifestation of unhealthy grief is self-pity. The Bible does not contain a specific reference to self-pity—we don't find it in any of the lists of sins recorded in the Epistles. However, it is at the root of many of the other sins which are specifically listed.[2] When we indulge in self-pity, we are expressing our lack of faith in the benevolent kindness of our heavenly Father. A sense of loss floods our lives and drowns out any sense that even in the most adverse circumstances, God loves us with an unchanging love.

Self-pity blunts our faith, saps our gratitude, and strangles our joy. It can also lead to a kind of warped pleasure when we revel in our own negative emotions. And we want others to share our pain too. Self-pity can become extremely manipulative as we draw our friends into the net of our misery and self-indulgence.

Abigail Dodds expresses it like this:

The problem of self-pity is a problem of sight. Self-pitying

---

2   As an example, read the story of Ahab and Naboth's vineyard (1 Kings 21) and look at the roots and fruits of self-pity.

people have not set the Lord before themselves as he really is—glorious, kind, sovereign, and just. They mainly have set themselves and their circumstances in their field of vision. Rather than crying out to God in our big and small moments of distress, self-pity would have us whimper in the misery of our own hearts.[3]

God's answer to self-pity is lamentation. We see this again and again in the psalms, particularly the psalms of David. On more than one occasion, David had reason to be sorry for himself. But he brought his genuine complaints to God. And there is no reticence or stoicism in his prayers:

How long, LORD? Will you forget me forever?
  How long will you hide your face from me?
How long must I wrestle with my thoughts
  and day after day have sorrow in my heart?
How long will my enemy triumph over me? (Ps. 13:1–2)

None of us can expect to live a lament-free life. So, how can we learn from David's example? What words should we use?

To learn the language of lament, we need to delve deeper into the psalms.

3   Abigail Dodds, "Woe Is Me: The Sin of Self-Pity and How to be Free," Desiring God, August 15, 2020.

Cries from the heart

The psalms cover every shade of human experience. They are passionate pastoral texts which focus on every mood of the human heart. John Calvin described the psalms as "an anatomy of all the parts of the soul."[4] Agony and ecstasy; exuberant joy and darkest despair; confession of sin and thankfulness for deliverance; explosions of praise and groans of agony—all of life is here. If we get to know the psalms well, we will have made one hundred and fifty friends for life. The psalms, forged in the crucible of real and often raw experience, meet us where we are.

As pastor and author Cole Feix observes,

The psalms are the nervous system of the Bible. They pervade the other 65 books and provide a sensory core for all of Scripture. All of the major biblical characters after Moses wrote, quoted, or worshipped to these holy hymns. The authors of the psalms span almost a thousand years and comprise an unlikely cast of characters. The styles of the psalms are vibrant and creative. There are poems, acrostics, narratives, and songs.[5]

In the Psalms we meet God in the praises of his people. Here theology becomes doxology. There are probably more direct statements about the character of God in the Psalms than in

---

4   John Calvin, "The Author's Preface," *Commentary on the Psalms*, vol. 1, James Anderson, trans. (*Christian Classics Ethereal Library*).

5   Cole Feix, "An Anatomy of All Parts of the Soul: A Guide to the Psalms," So We Speak, September 3, 2018.

any other book in the Bible. Here we meet God as Creator and Sustainer, as Saviour and Shepherd, as King and Warrior and Bridegroom. And of course this was the hymn book of Christ. As he sang these words, he came to understand that many of them would be fulfilled in his own life and ministry. As we read the psalms today, we hear the whisper of his voice and feel the touch of his hand.

And significantly for this book, at least a third of the psalms are laments.

Whet your appetite with the following verses:

O God, be not far from me; O my God, make haste to help me! (Ps. 71:12 ESV)

O Lord, all my longing is before you; my sighing is not hidden from you. My heart throbs; my strength fails me, and the light of my eyes—it also has gone from me. (Ps. 38:9–10 ESV)

From the end of the earth I call to you when my heart is faint. (Ps. 61:2 ESV)

I am weary with my crying out; my throat is parched. My eyes grow dim with waiting for my God. (Ps. 69:3 ESV)

I cry aloud to God, aloud to God, and he will hear me. In the day of my trouble I seek the Lord; in the night my hand is stretched out without wearying; my soul refuses to be comforted. (Ps. 77:1–2 ESV)

Be merciful to me, Lord, for I am in distress;
    my eyes grow weak with sorrow,
    my soul and body with grief.

My life is consumed by anguish
    and my years by groaning;
my strength fails because of my affliction,
    and my bones grow weak. (Ps. 31:9–12 NIV)

Lamenting versus grumbling

It may be helpful at this stage to address a concern which often arises when we think about lamentation—namely, how does lamenting differ from grumbling? When does the former become the latter, grieving the Holy Spirit and possibly leading to a hard heart?

One of the abiding sins into which Israel fell was grumbling against the Lord. We find multiple examples of this during their time in the wilderness. Immediately after the amazing deliverance at the Red Sea, we read,

The whole Israelite community set out from Elim and came to the Desert of Sin, which is between Elim and Sinai, on the fifteenth day of the second month after they had come out of Egypt. In the desert the whole community grumbled against Moses and Aaron. The Israelites said to them, "If only we had died by the Lord's hand in Egypt!

There we sat around pots of meat and ate all the food we wanted, but you have brought us out into this desert to starve this entire assembly to death." (Exod. 16:1–3)

This grumbling, an ungrateful and churlish whinging about God's provision, reveals an inexplicable amnesia. In Egypt they had experienced oppression and even genocide as every baby boy was killed (Exod. 1:15–22). God heard their cry for help and rescued them in the most miraculous way. Amazingly, their limited wilderness diet now caused them to forget their liberation—all that they could remember was the Egyptian cuisine. Further, by refusing to believe that God could provide for their needs in the journey ahead, they showed that they had forgotten how God had provided for them so far.

This was only one example of a negative pattern of behaviour God's people returned to again and again.[6]

Even though God had chastened them, they did not learn their lesson, and when they could find no water in Meribah, they complained again (Num. 20:1–13). Psalm 95 describes this rebellion, and the writer to the Hebrews references this psalm to warn about the dangers of grumbling (Heb. 3:7–19). The danger is that grumbling leads to a hardening of heart:

Today, if you hear his voice,
  do not harden your hearts
as you did in the rebellion,

6   See Numbers 11:1–4; 12:1; 14:1–2; 16:1–3,41; 20:3; 21:5.

during the time of testing in the wilderness,
where your ancestors tested and tried me,
　though for forty years they saw what I did.
That is why I was angry with that generation;
　I said, "Their hearts are always going astray,
　and they have not known my ways."
So I declared on oath in my anger,
　"They shall never enter my rest." (Heb. 3:7–11)

Such grumbling flows from "a sinful, unbelieving heart that turns away from the living God" (3:12). Behind the grumbling is unbelief that refuses to trust God's goodness, and this provokes his anger.

So is this grumbling the same as the complaints which we find in the Psalms?

No! The two must not be confused.

Grumbling is when our grief and anguish drive us from God rather than towards him. We become angry with God and blame him for our loss; comfort and ease become idols that we long for. Our resentment can easily harden into bitterness and a denial of God's goodness, a maligning of God's character. So we charge God with wrongdoing and refuse to trust him, in spite of his past mercies.

Lamenting, on the other hand, flies to God in desperation. It talks to God about our pain; it pours out our fears, frustrations, and sorrows. As a result, we are able to renew our confidence in God. Rather than denying our faith, our complaints are an expression of this very faith. It may not feel like it, but our anguished cries reveal a heart that is pursuing God, flying to God because we trust him. Our complaint is an appeal to God based on confidence in his character.

Remember Job? He brings a myriad of complaints before the Lord, but they flow from a heart that bows before him in desperate but honest faith:

> At this, Job got up and tore his robe and shaved his
> head. Then he fell to the ground in worship and said:
> > "Naked I came from my mother's womb,
> > and naked I will depart.
> > The LORD gave and the LORD has taken away;
> > may the name of the LORD be praised."
> In all this, Job did not sin by charging God with
> wrongdoing. (Job 1:20–22)

The language of lament: turn, tell, pray, trust

The laments in the Psalms are as varied as the experience of the author. Some are individual or personal. The psalmist often feels alone—deserted by God and man—and the psalm flows from this sense of isolation.[7] Other laments are inspired by national trials and written for the whole community to express their griefs before God.[8]

---

7   Individual laments include Psalm 3, 4, 5, 7, 9–10, 13, 14, 17, 22, 25, 26, 27, 28, 31, 36, 39, 40:12–17, 41, 42–43, 52, 53, 54, 55, 56, 57, 59, 61, 64, 70, 71, 77, 86, 89, 120, 139, 141, and 142.

8   Community laments include Psalm 12, 44, 58, 60, 74, 79, 80, 83, 85, 89, 90, 94, 123, 126, and 129.

In spite of the variety and variation, we can identify a common pattern in these psalms of lament. Most contain at least four elements:

Turn

The psalmist may feel isolated from God, but regardless of this, he deliberately seeks the face of God. This is the difference between faith and unbelief—grief can drive us towards God or drive us from him. The psalmist does not run from God—he runs towards him. Our first step therefore is to run to God.

Tell

The psalmist talks to God about how he feels. Every lament contains some form of complaint. This varies according to circumstances, but often it includes a sense of God's absence. Whatever else the psalmist may have lost, he knows that his greatest need is to know that God is with him still. He honestly identifies the pain, uncertainty, and anguish which may be raging in his soul. These complaints can sometimes border on intemperance, but, as we have seen, they flow from the soft heart of faith rather the hard, unbelieving heart.

Pray

Having voiced his complaints, the psalmist then begins to turn them into intercessory prayer. There is a change in the direction of his heart as he reaches out to God in humble request. This is why lament does not lead him to despair. As Vroegop explains,

Despair lives under the hopeless resignation that God doesn't care, he doesn't hear, and nothing is ever going to change.[9]

As Christians, we know that God is a faithful Father, so we do not have to live in despair! We can approach his throne "in our time of need" (Heb. 4:16). We may not receive an immediate answer, but we still persist in our prayers to him.

Trust

Almost every lament in the Psalms ends with an expression of trust.[10] By this we see that the exercise of lament has the outcome of faith. The laments themselves exhibit a definite movement from darkness to light; this should be the destination for our laments too. Faith grows and hope is reborn as we honestly confess our needs to God. Faith involves more than intellectual assent, as Jerry Bridges has observed:

Trust is not a passive state of mind. It is a vigorous act of the soul by which we choose to lay hold on the promises of God and cling to them despite the adversity that at times seeks to overwhelm us.[11]

---

9 Vroegop, *Dark Clouds, Deep Mercy*, 16. A similar four-part breakdown of the psalms of lamentation appears in a number of places; the first place I came across it is in the writings of Mark Vroegop.

10 The only exception is Psalm 88, which appears to begin and end in the darkness.

11 Jerry Bridges, *Trusting God, Even When Life Hurts* (Colorado Springs, CO: NavPress, 2008), 214.

In this sense lamenting involves a journey—a journey from desolation to delight. Often the circumstances which provoked the lament have not changed, but the heart of the lamenter has been renewed.

So what does this look like for us?

Lamenting when the wicked prosper

Psalm 10 does not have a specific heading like some other psalms do. In some ways this is fitting, because the questions it raises are timeless.

Turn

The previous psalm reminded us that God reigns in justice:

> The LORD reigns forever;
>> he has established his throne for judgment.
> He rules the world in righteousness
>> and judges the peoples with equity. (Ps. 9:7–8)

But in Psalm 10 there appears to be no evidence of this: the psalmist sees terrible injustice all around him, and God seems so far away. And yet the psalmist turns his heart to God and begins to pour out his heart to him:

> Why, LORD, do you stand far off?
>> Why do you hide yourself in times of trouble? (10:1)

Notice that he does not run from God—he runs towards him.

There is an irony here. He feels God's absence, yet he trusts that God is listening. His faith may be weak, but it triumphs over his emotions and fears.

Tell

The psalmist begins to tell God about what is troubling him. He has already articulated the fact that he feels God is far away. Now he describes the particular issue which distresses him. The wicked oppress the innocent and get away with it. Their hearts are full of arrogance:

> In his arrogance the wicked man hunts down the weak,
>> who are caught in the schemes he devises. (v. 2)

The wicked man's contempt for the weak stems from his contempt for God:

> In his pride the wicked man does not seek him;
>> in all his thoughts there is no room for God. (v. 4)

And yet he prospers!

> His ways are always prosperous;
>> your laws are rejected by him;
>> he sneers at all his enemies. (v. 5)

He is vicious and treacherous (vv. 7–9), confident that he can do what he likes without any fear of recriminations or divine intervention:

> His victims are crushed, they collapse;
> they fall under his strength.
> He says to himself, "God will never notice;
> he covers his face and never sees." (vv. 10–11)

The psalmist complains because this is not the way things should be. How can God allow this? Doesn't he see? Doesn't he care?

Notice how he offers a detailed description of the problem. Our complaints may be very different, but we are encouraged to follow the psalmist's example and lay them honestly before our God.

Pray

The psalmist's lament now turns into prayer as he pleads with God to step in and deal with this injustice and evil. There are still questions, but the mood has changed:

> Arise, Lord! Lift up your hand, O God.
> Do not forget the helpless. (v. 12)

The picture is of a warrior lifting up his hand in battle. The psalmist begs God to come and defend the defenceless—to act on behalf of the weak and exploited. His prayer is very specific:

> Break the arm of the wicked man;

call the evildoer to account for his wickedness
that would not otherwise be found out. (v. 15)

This may sound harsh in our ears, but the psalmist is not seeking to take the matter into his own hands: "Vengeance is mine, thus says the Lord" (see Rom. 12:19). Rather, he is trusting in the justice and righteousness of God to put things right. "Break[ing] the arm of the wicked" means breaking their power to oppress. A just God will take care of this.

Trust

Having poured out his heart before the Lord, the psalmist ends by expressing his confidence in God:

The LORD is King for ever and ever;
    the nations will perish from his land.
You, LORD, hear the desire of the afflicted;
    you encourage them, and you listen to their cry,
defending the fatherless and the oppressed,
    so that mere earthly mortals
    will never again strike terror. (vv. 16–18)

It is not clear whether or not the psalmist ever saw the earthly outcome of his prayer, but he is confident that, whether now or in the future, God will put things right.

Psalm 10 is just one example of a personal lament, but most of the psalms were forged in the crucible of pain and suffering. They are one of God's most precious gifts to his people, giving us a language we can use when our own words fail.

We need to learn the language of lament so that we too can "turn, tell, pray, and trust."

Questions

1. When is anger right? When is it wrong? How can we tell the difference?
2. "Failure to lament is dangerous for our emotional and spiritual wellbeing and may lead to toxic emotions such as bitterness, envy, self-pity and unbelief." How does a failure to lament lead to these toxic emotions? Why is self-pity so destructive, and how do we overcome it?
3. Read Hebrews 3:7–19. How do we avoid a hard heart and grumbling lips?
4. Work through Psalm 13 and decipher the "turn, tell, pray, and trust" pattern. How might this become a pattern for your own lament?

4

Learning Core
Truths

I owe Robin a great deal.

My Bible class teacher during my teenage years, he instilled in me a love for, and confidence in, the Bible as the Word of God. Having said that, Robin could sometimes be rather unconventional.

One year, just before Christmas, he issued us a challenge I have never forgotten:

If you want to be strong Christians when you grow up, you need to get to know the whole of the Bible. It stands to reason that if God gave us the whole book, he wants us to read the whole book. So why not decide that next year you are going to read the whole Bible from cover to cover? I'll give you ten reasons to do so …

Robin did just that. I have to confess that I cannot remember most of them. However, one made a huge impression on me:

One day, when you get to heaven, you will see this tall man with a long white beard. He will come across to you and will say, "Hello. My name is Habakkuk. Did you enjoy reading my book?" And if you haven't read it, you will be really embarrassed.

I told you Robin was slightly unconventional!

But the point struck home. I didn't want to be embarrassed. That afternoon I tried reading Habakkuk. I was twelve at the time, and I'm not sure what I made of the book. It seemed that the prophet was confused and could not understand what God was doing. However, by the end he had come to trust God, and I was thrilled to discover his final words, which I already knew from a popular chorus we used to sing:

Though the fig tree does not bud
    and there are no grapes on the vines,
though the olive crop fails
    and the fields produce no food,
though there are no sheep in the pen
    and no cattle in the stalls,
yet I will rejoice in the LORD,
    I will be joyful in God my Savior. (Hab. 3:17–18)

What I did not know then was that this book is a wonderful example of biblical lamentation.

Living by faith

What we find in Habakkuk is the same pattern of lamentation we have discovered in many other places. It is a dialogue between God and his faithful but confused servant. The prophet knows that God is infinitely powerful and impeccably just and good. But what he actually sees seems to contradict this. So in the face of moral decay within Israel and the rise of an aggressive and expansionist Babylonian Empire, Habakkuk is bewildered. And consequently, he laments God's apparent inactivity and unconcern:

> How long, LORD, must I call for help,
>   but you do not listen?
> Or cry out to you, "Violence!"
>   but you do not save?
> Why do you make me look at injustice?
>   Why do you tolerate wrongdoing? (1:2–3)

Confusion and disappointment do not make him turn away from God. Rather, Habakkuk intentionally turns *towards* God and tells him about his dilemma. Every lament features some kind of complaint, and Habakkuk's is no exception.

When God responds by telling the prophet that he is going to chasten his people by crushing them under the wheels of the ruthless and vicious Babylonian superpower (1:5–11), this raises even more complaints. Understandably! How can a holy God justify using such evil people? Surely the cure is worse than the disease?

Your eyes are too pure to look on evil;
  you cannot tolerate wrongdoing.
Why then do you tolerate the treacherous?
  Why are you silent while the wicked
  swallow up those more righteous than themselves? (1:13)

Candidly, Habakkuk tells God that what he has heard does not seem to fit with what he knows about God's character and purposes.

God's response? A promise that he will work out his purposes in his own time, and that in the end Habakkuk will see that God's perfect wisdom, justice, and goodness will be vindicated (2:2–20).

God summons the prophet to faith:

The LORD replied …

See, the enemy is puffed up;
  his desires are not upright—
  but the righteous person will live by his faithfulness. (2:3)

In spite of appearances,

The LORD is in his holy temple;
  let all the earth be silent before him. (2:20)

Habakkuk responds by praying for God to act:

Lord, I have heard of your fame;
   I stand in awe of your deeds, Lord.
Repeat them in our day,
   in our time make them known;
   in wrath remember mercy. (3:2)

He ends his book with a psalm of praise (3:1–19), expressing confidence in God's steadfastness:

The Sovereign Lord is my strength;
   he makes my feet like the feet of a deer,
   he enables me to tread on the heights. (v. 19)

The prophet has moved from lamentation to confident faith—from "why?" to worship. All the elements of classic lament are found here: he turns, he tells, he prays, and he trusts.

At the heart of this prophetic book is a fresh understanding of who God is. And this surely is one of the main purposes and benefits of lamentation. Remember Elisabeth Elliot (chapter 1), who gained a new understanding of God through her excruciating grief?

Lament always rises from a place of faith. We don't struggle with questions about God's character unless we've believed in his greatness and goodness in the first place. In lament we deepen our theological grasp. But it is a theology forged in the fires of affliction. Here we learn to rehearse and discover anew the great certainties of our faith.

The stability of objective truth

Grief and loss can confuse us and derail our theology. There seems to be such a gap between faith and experience.

Our problem today is that we have a shallow view of God. We long for simple solutions and seek security in simplicity. But the truth is that when it comes to the knowledge of God, the truth shelters in the depths. We are to love and worship God with our minds, but our greatest need of all is to behold the fathomless beauty of the Lord:

> One thing I ask from the Lord,
>   this only do I seek:
> that I may dwell in the house of the Lord
>   all the days of my life,
> to gaze on the beauty of the Lord
>   and to seek him in his temple. (Ps. 27:4)

Listen to the eighteenth-century preacher and theologian Jonathan Edwards:

> The redeemed have all their *objective* good in God. God Himself is the great good which they are brought to the possession and enjoyment of by redemption. He is the highest good, and the sum of all that good which Christ purchased. God is the inheritance of the saints; He is the portion of their souls. God is their wealth and treasure, their food, their life, their dwelling place, their ornament and diadem, and their everlasting honour and glory. They

have none in heaven but God.

He is the great good which the redeemed are received to at death, and which they are to rise to at the end of the world. The Lord God, He is the light of the heavenly Jerusalem, and is the "river of the water of life" that runs, and the tree of life that grows, "in the midst of the paradise of God."

The glorious excellencies and beauty of God will be what will forever entertain the minds of the saints, and the love of God will be their everlasting feast. The redeemed will indeed enjoy other things. They will enjoy the angels and will enjoy one another: but that which they shall enjoy in the angels, or each other, or in anything else whatsoever, that will yield them delight and happiness, will be what will be seen of God in them.[1]

It is as the lamenting soul honestly brings its complaints to God that it comes to a fuller and richer view of who God is. Our theology is refined, our hopes are deepened, and our vision is purified. Like Habakkuk, we move from "why?" to worship.

In this process we rediscover three great truths about our magnificent triune God:

- The Lord is sovereign and reigns over all; we are in his

---

1 Jonathan Edwards, "God Glorified in the Work of Redemption, by the Greatness of Man's Dependence upon Him, in the Whole of It (1731)," in *The Sermons of Jonathan Edwards: A Reader*, ed. Wilson H. Kimnach, Kenneth P. Minkema, and Douglas A. Sweeney (New Haven, CT: Yale University Press, 1999), 74–75.

hands. Loss does not take him by surprise but is part of his purpose for us.

- The Lord is good, and he always means his people well.
- God is wise, and he does all things well.

God is sovereign, and he reigns over all

We have seen that when we lament, it is tempting to doubt that God is really in control. Perhaps he is not what we thought he was. Maybe he is a kind of "absentee landlord" who made the world and then retreated into glorious isolation. We lapse into a kind of *Star Wars* theology: good (God) may be stronger than evil (the devil), but it is a close-run thing. Sometimes evil will have the ascendancy. Trouble takes God by surprise, and he grieves and wrings his hands in frustrated impotence. He sees his plans thwarted and his desires blocked, but there is little he can do about it.

And so we reason: if I have to surrender either God's goodness and kindness or his sovereignty and power, surely it is better to jettison the latter rather than the former?

Recently my younger daughter Emmaus celebrated her thirtieth birthday. My wife Edrie and I, along with the rest of the family, rejoiced with her. But our feelings were bittersweet. Edrie had become seriously ill during the pregnancy all those years ago and has been in a wheelchair ever since. Intense pain is still her daily companion: she has not gone a single night without it for more years than we care to remember. We have often wept and lamented together. Seeing my wife in such anguish is difficult and has often caused me to struggle with my faith.

I have been encouraged by the kind and timely words of so many people and have experienced God's warm embrace through his people. But there have been those who, with the most benevolent intentions, have said things which were unhelpful and damaging. In particular, they have occasionally encouraged me to adopt a less all-embracing view of God's sovereignty.

But the truth is that God is powerful and at work in his world. He is not the "absentee landlord" described above. Yet he will never overturn human decisions and choices. We are not puppets, and sometimes our actions can trump and frustrate his purposes. That explains why there are wars and rumours of wars (Matt. 24:6). Humankind is a blight on the planet. The environmental crisis is man-made. God looks on with frustration, but he will not step in to reverse man's wickedness. When we suffer painful loss, we cannot blame God. He has nothing to do with it.

But how does all this apply to Edrie's illness, which is clearly not man-made? One possibility is that a less-than-sovereign God is bound by my choices and decisions, so he may want to heal my wife, but he is bound by my lack of faith. If only I could boost my faith, then God could act. Once I reach the threshold level, God's considerable resources can come into play.

This may sound comforting—I just need to strive a little harder. But in the end, it is devastating. It is not faith in God, but faith in faith. Faith becomes the tool by which I manipulate God and force his hand rather than a cry of desperation and weakness: "I believe; help my unbelief" (see Mark 9:24).

The surrender of God's sovereignty is too great a price to pay in order to find a superficial answer to a profound problem.

And it is pastorally disastrous. One of my greatest comforts over the last thirty years has been to know that however painful our lives have been, we are in God's hands. And I don't want to be anywhere else.

What's more, the surrender of God's sovereignty is biblically unfaithful. According to Scripture, God has an eternal, all-embracing plan which cannot be defeated and will ultimately result in his glory and the good of his people. God reigns over all creation, and his will is the final explanation of all things. It was the pagan king Nebuchadnezzar who confessed,

At the end of that time, I, Nebuchadnezzar, raised my eyes toward heaven, and my sanity was restored. Then I praised the Most High; I honored and glorified him who lives forever.

His dominion is an eternal dominion;
  his kingdom endures from generation to generation.
All the peoples of the earth
  are regarded as nothing.
He does as he pleases
  with the powers of heaven
  and the peoples of the earth.
No one can hold back his hand
  or say to him: "What have you done?"

At the same time that my sanity was restored, my honor and splendor were returned to me for the glory of my kingdom. My advisers and nobles sought me out, and I was restored to my throne and became even greater than before. (Dan. 4:34–36)

Notice that it was when the king recognized that it was God and not he himself who reigned that his sanity was restored. It is the height of foolishness to try to live in God's world without acknowledging that he is Lord of all.

None of this is to deny human responsibility and the integrity of our choices. What we do counts, and what we decide determines our lives. God's sovereignty never minimizes or restricts our responsibility. So we make real choices—we love, we hate, we rebel, and we submit, but this never lessens God's sovereignty.

This has been the softest of the three pillows on which Edrie and I have rested our heads.

God is good, all the way through

Or perhaps God isn't as good as we thought he was? How can a good God tolerate cancer or child abuse or exploitation? Maybe he is in control, but he just doesn't care. Like the Greek gods, he is capricious. If not, how could he create a world which is so full of misery and wickedness and grief? Or maybe he is just plain incompetent? He meant the world to be good, but somehow got it wrong?

In the words of William Shakespeare:

As flies to wanton boys are we to th' gods,

They kill us for their sport.[2]

Here in *King Lear*, one of Shakespeare's most brutal tragedies, the pagan Duke of Gloucester, who has been betrayed and blinded by his own son, has a theological explanation for his suffering. The gods are capricious and spiteful. They are as wanton as little boys who enjoy pulling the wings off flies just for the fun of it. The gods are like immature, unkind children, and man is as insignificant as the flies they crush.

Even in our darkest days, we may never entertain such a harsh view of God. However, as we saw earlier, when our hearts our breaking, there seems to be a real discrepancy between what we have known of God's goodness and the way he seems to be treating us now. We batter the gates of heaven with our cries for help, but God is silent. When times are good we taste his kindness in a million ways, and yet when the bottom falls out of our worlds, he is nowhere to be found.

This was at the heart of Habakkuk's lament. How can a good God allow bad things to happen? How can he use evil people to bring about his purposes?[3] How can he tolerate treacherous people? How can he be silent in the face of evil? How can we trust him when he appears to be acting out of character?

This seems to be at the heart of Job's lament too. His pain is so intense, and it is at God's hands. Why is there such a disparity between past and present experience?

---

2   William Shakespeare, *King Lear*, 4.1.36–37.

3   Hab. 1:2–4, 13–17.

If only my anguish could be weighed
    and all my misery be placed on the scales!
It would surely outweigh the sand of the seas—
    no wonder my words have been impetuous.
The arrows of the Almighty are in me,
    my spirit drinks in their poison;
  God's terrors are marshaled against me. (Job 6:2–4)

How do we respond to this? What do we mean when we say that the Lord is "good"?

We may define the word "good" as meaning "worthy of approval." This means that everything God does is worthy of approval. Always. His character, his decisions, his plans, and his purposes. All his actions are determined by his goodness. We may not be able to see it now, but one day it will be abundantly clear.

God's action is determined by his character. He is not free to sin or to lie or to perpetrate an "ungood" deed. He does everything he *wants* to do. And what he wants to do will always be that which is worthy of approval. God's goodness is manifested in his mercy, grace, and patience.

God's goodness is his glory.

When Moses asks to see God's glory, the Lord hides him in a rock. Then, God manifests and declares his glory:

And he passed in front of Moses, proclaiming, "The LORD, the LORD, the compassionate and gracious God, slow to anger, abounding in love and faithfulness, maintaining love to thousands, and forgiving wickedness, rebellion and sin. Yet he does not leave the guilty unpunished; he punishes the children and their children for the sin of the parents to the third and fourth generation." (Exod. 34:6–7)

This will become a kind of Old Testament credal statement.[4] Moses rehearses it just before his death:

He is the Rock, his works are perfect,
    and all his ways are just.
A faithful God who does no wrong,
    upright and just is he. (Deut. 32:4)

The psalmist invites us to discover it for ourselves: "Taste and see that the LORD is good" (Ps. 34:8).

James reminds us that every good thing we enjoy now has come from the good hand of God:

Every good and perfect gift is from above, coming down from the Father of the heavenly lights, who does not change like shifting shadows. (James 1:17)

Scripture constantly asserts this:

For the LORD is good and his love endures forever;

4   Compare Ps. 103:8; Joel 2:13; Jonah 4:2.

his faithfulness continues through all generations.
(Ps. 100:5)

The LORD is good to all;
he has compassion on all he has made. (Ps. 145:9)

Of course, the greatest revelation of the goodness of God is Calvary:

You see, at just the right time, when we were still powerless, Christ died for the ungodly. Very rarely will anyone die for a righteous person, though for a good person someone might possibly dare to die. But God demonstrates his own love for us in this: While we were still sinners, Christ died for us. (Rom. 5:6–8)

A wise old Christian once said to me, "If you ever doubt God's love, go back to the cross. Turn your eyes to Calvary. Stay close to Jesus."

The cross reveals the awesome majesty of God's holiness in his antipathy to sin and his unflinching commitment to justice. It also reveals the indescribable love of God. Just think of who he gave, and of the terrible suffering he gave him to, and of the rebels for whom the gift was given. The cross is the final and definitive triumph of justice *and* love.

In our darkest days, Edrie and I have found the pillow of God's goodness a comfortable place on which to rest our weary heads.

The secret things belong to him

My elder daughter wanted a hamster when she was little. I had resisted requests for pets, but she persisted. So we made an agreement. She could have a hamster as long as I could give it a name. She agreed, and I suggested the name of one of Isaiah's sons: "Maher-Shalal-Hash-Baz" (Isa. 8:1–3). I thought this would put her off. But no, it didn't. She got her hamster. And he got a nickname: "Twinkle"!

One day someone left the cage door open, and we never saw Twinkle again. Somewhere under the floorboards in a house in Worcester lie the bones of a hamster with a magnificent name!

Twinkle had a happy, if short, life. But his experience was confined to the tiny world of his cage. He had a wheel to play on; he was fed and watered every day; he seemed to be content. What did he know of my world? I can love and hope and dream and worship. I can talk to people on the other side of the world without moving from my desk. I can make decisions that may be wise or foolish, and with long-term consequences.

Twinkle knew nothing of this. If it were possible for hamsters to recognize such a thing as mystery, then he would be mystified. Why? Because there is an immense gap between the mind of a hamster and the mind of a human.

But how much greater, then, is the gap between the mind of God and the human mind? In our arrogance, we create a God in our own image and then get agitated when we cannot understand all his actions. We may be able to see the corners in the "jigsaws" of our lives, but we cannot see the full picture.

We've seen that God is sovereign; we've seen that God is good.

But there is a third pillow on which we can rest our heads when we are in the dark place of lamentation: *God is wise*. We can share in this wisdom if we begin with the perspective of the fear of the Lord (Prov. 1:7). And his wisdom will always far exceed ours. In his grace, he has revealed everything we *need* to know, even though it might not be everything we might *want* to know:

> The secret things belong to the Lord our God, but the things revealed belong to us and to our children forever, that we may follow all the words of this law. (Deut. 29:29)

At the climax of the book of Job, God does not give his faithful servant a clear and simple answer to the scores of questions that he has bombarded heaven with. Instead, he displays his glory before Job and asks *him* a series of questions, which Job cannot answer (Job 38–41). As far as we know, Job never gets the full picture containing the causes of his suffering. God is not being mean to Job or trying to belittle him. He will soon affirm and restore him (Job 42). What God is doing is leading Job to recognise that there are limits to his human understanding. Only God knows all things from beginning to end; he looks at things from an eternal perspective. His wisdom means that he always chooses the best goals, and also the best means of achieving those goals.

Job's comforters were controlled by a water-tight theology which had no place for mystery. The message of the book of Job is that lamentation is the proper response in the face of the overwhelming mystery of suffering. We too lament in the face of painful and inexplicable mystery. We rightly affirm God's sovereignty, goodness, and wisdom. How then can we begin to understand the mysteries of providence? Lamentation itself becomes the language of humble wonder. In the words of Tom Wright:

It is no part of the Christian vocation, then, to be able to explain what's happening and why. In fact, it *is* part of the Christian vocation *not to be able* to explain—and to lament instead. As the Spirit laments within us, so we become, even in our self-isolation, small shrines where the presence and healing love of God can dwell.[5]

So, lamenting is one of the most theologically informed actions we can take.

In our garden at home, we have a bench which our children bought for us. Inscribed on it are words which have become a kind of motto for Edrie and me over the years, made up of just a fragment of one verse: "God's way is perfect" (see Ps. 18:30).

In the midst of lamentation, we have learned that we can rest our weary heads on three pillows:

God is *sovereign*. Whatever happens, we are in his hands. Nothing comes under his radar or takes him by surprise.

God is *good*. He is too kind to hurt us unnecessarily. When we doubt this, we flee to the cross and drink again at the fountain of

---

5   N. T. Wright, "Christianity Offers No Answers About the Coronavirus. It's Not Supposed To," *Time*, March 29, 2020.

his mercy. We may not see his hand, but we can trust his heart.

God is *wise*. He is too wise to make mistakes. When we cannot comprehend his purposes, we can still trust that he knows exactly what he is doing. One day we will look back and see that it was perfect.

This is the place where lamenting Habakkuk also sheltered:

Lord, are you not from everlasting?
  My God, my Holy One, you will never die.
You, Lord, have appointed them to execute judgment;
  you, my Rock, have ordained them to punish. (1:12)

When I meet Habakkuk in heaven, I will say, "Thank you!"

Questions

1. Read Habakkuk 1. What is the basis of Habakkuk's lamentation? In the midst of it, he reflects on God's character. What does he affirm (1:12–13)?

2. Someone might claim, "Trouble takes God by surprise, and he grieves and wrings his hands in frustrated impotence. He sees his plans thwarted and his desires blocked, but there is little he can do about it." How is this statement wrong, and unhelpful when we are lamenting?

3. Read Psalm 100. The psalmist affirms God's goodness (v. 5). How should this affect the way we approach God today? (vv. 1–4)

4. How does the cross of Christ reveal God's sovereignty, his goodness, and his wisdom? Why is this so important when

we lament? (See Acts 2:22–24; Rom. 5:6–8; 1 Cor. 1:18–25)

5. What other attributes of God help us to lament well in the midst of loss?

6. Author and theologian Michael Horton once observed, "Theology is [not like preparing for a school exam]. It is a matter of life and death. … It's about living, and dying, well."[6] Do you agree? How might the truths in this chapter help you to live and die well?

6 Michael Horton, *A Place for Weakness: Preparing Yourself for Suffering* (Grand Rapids: Zondervan, 2006), 19.

5

Learning
Trust

When David wrote Psalm 56, he was terrified.

The inscription at the beginning tells us that he wrote this psalm "when the Philistines has seized him in Gath." (Read the background in 1 Samuel 21.) After his victory over Goliath, David had become the commander of the armies of Israel.

His success in this role caused the women of Israel to compose a rather exaggerated ditty, comparing him to King Saul: "As they danced, they sang: 'Saul has slain his thousands, and David his tens of thousands'" (1 Sam. 18:7).

As you can imagine, this did not please Saul. His jealousy soon turned to paranoia, and he tried to kill David on more than one occasion. Running for his life, David seemed to have lost everything—his position, his home, his reputation, and even his wife.

David's life was under constant threat, and it was probably during this period that he wrote many of his laments—perhaps Psalm 10 (which we considered earlier), for instance. In fact,

David's situation became so perilous that he made what might be considered a bizarre decision: to take refuge among his enemies and to seek asylum with Achish, king of Gath:

That day David fled from Saul and went to Achish king of Gath. But the servants of Achish said to him, "Isn't this David, the king of the land? Isn't he the one they sing about in their dances:

'Saul has slain his thousands,
   and David his tens of thousands?'"

David took these words to heart and was very much afraid of Achish king of Gath. So he pretended to be insane in their presence; and while he was in their hands he acted like a madman, making marks on the doors of the gate and letting saliva run down his beard.

Achish said to his servants, "Look at the man! He is insane! Why bring him to me? Am I so short of madmen that you have to bring this fellow here to carry on like this in front of me? Must this man come into my house?" (1 Sam. 21:10–15)

The people of Gath knew David's reputation all too well. Goliath had been the city's champion (1 Sam. 17:4), How many of the residents had lost family members—fathers, husbands, son, brothers—to David's sword? So David has a target on his back. He is public enemy number one! As the servants of Achish remind the king of this, David takes it to heart. No wonder he is terrified.

Two responses to terror

In response to his terror, David does two things.

First, he comes up with a cunning plan to feign madness and deflect attention. Slobbering and scratching the door, he convinces the king that he is insane. Achish is revolted by this pathetic and helpless creature. He concludes that David obviously poses no threat to Gath anymore, and so, in disgust, the king has David removed from his sight.

David escapes, and in gratitude to God for his deliverance, he writes Psalm 34:

> I will extol the LORD at all times;
>> his praise will always be on my lips.
> I will glory in the LORD;
>> let the afflicted hear and rejoice.
> Glorify the LORD with me;
>> let us exalt his name together.
> I sought the Lord, and he answered me;
>> he delivered me from all my fears. (Ps. 34:1–4)[1]

But while still in Gath, David did a second thing. He wrote a lament to bring his concerns to God, one recorded for us in

---

1 The Abimelech mentioned in the inscription is an alternative name for Achish. The psalm refers to the same incident.

Psalm 56. This describes David's journey from fear to faith; from light to darkness; from the jaws of death to joy in God's presence.

As we examine this psalm, we discover (yet again) that lamenting is one experience God uses to mature us in our trust in him.

We have discovered that there is a clear pattern in the psalms of lament: turn, tell, pray, and trust, and we find these four elements in Psalm 56. David turns to God and asks for mercy (v. 1). He tells God about the things that trouble him (vv. 2, 6–7). He prays for God to remember his trials and remove his enemies (vv. 8–9). He expresses his trust in the Lord (vv. 3–4, 9–13).

Honest confession

First, observe David's honesty before God. He begins by turning his heart to God: "Be merciful to me, my God …" (56:1).

David does not boast of his righteousness or try to bargain with God. Rather, he begins by crying out for mercy. He knows that he needs God, and that if the Lord were to remove his hand, he would fall flat on his face. This is not hyperbole. David's life is literally in the balance.

He then brings his complaints to the Lord, spelling out his circumstances:

> for my enemies are in hot pursuit;
>> all day long they press their attack.
> My adversaries pursue me all day long;
>> in their pride many are attacking me. (vv. 1–2)

The enemies David refers to here could be either Saul or the Philistines, but he is probably referring to both of them. It feels as if everyone is against him! His enemies are in "hot pursuit"; they have their hands around his throat; they are threatening to crush the life out of him. All day long they never let up. He wakes each morning with a sick feeling: Will I survive today? He has multiple foes, and he recognizes that it is their pride which drives them to hate and attack him:

> All day long they twist my words;
>   all their schemes are for my ruin.
> They conspire, they lurk,
>   they watch my steps,
>   hoping to take my life. (vv. 5–6)

Sometimes their assaults are physical, but they also attack him verbally, twisting and perverting and distorting his words, pouring scorn and derision on his head, and weaving a web of lies. They conspire against his life. Their ambition is clear—they want him dead!

So David has multiple enemies who are malicious, violent, devious, and persistent. The pressure is unrelenting and overwhelming. David feels alone and isolated. These are not phantom fears, but real and ever-present. Twice in the psalm, David tells us that he is experiencing fear (vv. 3, 11).

The confession of his fears is a good corrective to the superficial triumphalism, noted earlier, that sometimes shapes our thinking in unhealthy ways. Some Christians claim that they never have doubts or fears, never blink in the face of danger or loss. Most of us are not like that, though, for we know only too well that we are not in control of our lives. Like Job, we cannot protect our possessions, our family, and our health from the uncertainties of life. All of us are vulnerable, and our fear has an active imagination.

And in this we are not alone. The words which David used could well have been used by Jesus too. He also faced malicious, violent, devious, and persistent enemies. He experienced unrelenting and overwhelming pressure. In the end, he was utterly alone.

Think of his words just days before the cross:

Now my soul is troubled, and what shall I say? "Father, save me from this hour"? No, it was for this very reason I came to this hour. Father, glorify your name! (John 12:27–28)

Jesus uses these words to describe an intense sense of unease and apprehension as he approaches the horrors of Calvary. We will explore the lamentation of Jesus later (chapter 7), but for now, suffice it to notice that he also pours out his heart to his Father. In his human nature, he experiences the crushing weight of horror. Unlike David, though, he does not escape from danger. This helps us to appreciate the sheer courage of the Son of God, who was willing to pay the ultimate price for the redemption of his people.

It also encourages us yet again to share our fears with our heavenly Father, turning our fears into prayers:

Because of their wickedness do not let them escape;
   in your anger, God, bring the nations down. (Ps. 56:7)

David is not being vindictive here, but he is clearly placing the matter in God's hands. His enemies have acted in an unprovoked and malicious way, and before both Saul and Achish his conscience is clean. God's character is his place of refuge: God is holy, hating wickedness. He will vindicate his servant and defeat his enemies. As the Lord's anointed king, David can have confidence that this is God's will. His prayer is therefore in line with God's purposes.

But we may well ask the question: Didn't God know all these things already? Didn't he know David's troubles? Wasn't he aware of the unjust pursuit by Saul, the dangers posed by the Philistines, and the very real threats to David's life? Didn't God know how fear was gripping David's heart?

Of course the answer is "yes"—and David knew it too! Listen to what he writes in Psalm 139, where he confesses that God knows both his heart and his circumstances:

You have searched me, LORD,
   and you know me.
You know when I sit and when I rise;
   you perceive my thoughts from afar. (Ps. 139:1–2)

So, what is the point of telling God what he already knows? It is probable here that pressure has forced David to forget what God knows. Lamenting helps us to articulate our condition before God. As we have seen already, it helps us to be honest and to put our fears into words. But it does more than that. It helps us to remember what we know but might easily forget—that God already knows these things, and I can trust him for the future. So, lamenting is theologically therapeutic. Humbly laying our complaints before God is part of our journey to prayer and trust.

We now move on to the next stage of this journey.

Humble confidence

David is honest as he confesses his fears, but the overwhelming emphasis in this psalm is his confidence in the Lord:

> When I am afraid, I put my trust in you.
>   In God, whose word I praise—
> in God I trust and am not afraid.
>   What can mere mortals do to me? (Ps. 56:3–4)

> In God, whose word I praise,
>   in the LORD, whose word I praise—
> in God I trust and am not afraid.
>   What can man do to me? (vv. 10–11)

Through the process of lamenting, David moves from the admission of fear to the affirmation of faith. Notice how he focuses on God: "When I am afraid, I put my trust in you" (v. 3).

There is something quite deliberate here. It is as if David takes himself by the scruff of the neck and purposefully begins to bring God into the picture. At this point he is not talking to

God—but talking to himself, taking himself in hand. Speaking in the context of depression, Dr. Martyn Lloyd-Jones expressed it in this way:

Have you realized that most of your unhappiness in life is due to the fact that you are listening to yourself instead of talking to yourself?[2]

Referring to Psalm 42, he says,

Now this man's treatment was this: instead of allowing this self to talk to him, he starts talking to himself. "Why art thou cast down, O my soul?" he asks. His soul had been depressing him, crushing him. So he stands up and says, "Self, listen for moment, I will speak to you."[3]

Likewise, we sometimes need to preach to ourselves:

You must turn on yourself, upbraid yourself, condemn yourself, exhort yourself, and say to yourself: "Hope thou in God"—instead of muttering in this depressed, unhappy way. And then you must go on to remind yourself of God, Who God is, and what God is and what God has done, and what God has pledged Himself to do.

Then having done that, end on this great note: defy

---

2   Martyn Lloyd-Jones, *Spiritual Depression: Its Causes and Its Cure* (Grand Rapids: Eerdmans, 1965), 20.

3   Lloyd-Jones, *Spiritual Depression*, 21.

yourself, and defy other people, and defy the devil and the whole world, and say with this man: "I shall yet praise Him for the help of His countenance, who is also the health of my countenance and my God."[4]

One of the benefits of bringing our complaints before God is that it becomes a process in which we participate and begin to argue ourselves towards faith. Prayer, in this context, is simply laying out our fears before God.

Incidentally, you will notice that David repeats himself twice, saying almost identical things (vv. 3–4, 10–11). Perhaps this is because faith zigzags. We bring our concerns to God and think we've moved on. But we forget and later on need to repeat the process.

The result of all of this is that David begins to trust in the Lord. What is the origin of his trust? Where does he find the words with which to remonstrate with himself? Three times in these verses he praises God for his Word; David's confidence springs from the solid foundation of Scripture. Faith is not fallible conjecture or wishful thinking, but simply taking God at his Word. The Bible refreshes the psalmist's soul, gives joy to his heart, and brings light to his eyes (Ps. 19:7–9).

In his hands, on his heart

What does David discover when he comes to Scripture?

4   Lloyd-Jones, *Spiritual Depression*, 21.

Two great certainties turn his paralysing fear into audacious faith.

First, he knows that in spite of appearances, he is not in the hands of men, but in the hands of God. Twice he asks the same question: "What can mere mortals do to me?" (Ps. 56:4), and "What can man do to me?" (v. 11).

We might be tempted to answer, "A lot!" Remember the situation in Gath? But David is not being naive here. Yes, he is surrounded by enemies, but in the end, it is God who calls the shots. We are not in control—but God is! Remember what we learned in chapter 4? The sovereignty of God is the softest pillow on which we can rest our heads at night.

You may remember Terry Waite. Sent to Lebanon to negotiate the release of hostages, he was himself taken captive and held in solitary confinement for almost five years. On his release, he was asked about his faith while in the hands of men of violence. His response is reminiscent of David's in Psalm 56:

> If I can put it very, very simply—and this may seem too simple for some—I could say this in the face of my captors: you have the power to break my body, and you have tried; you have the power to bend my mind, and you have tried; but my soul is not yours to possess. There was that essential belief that my soul lay in the hands of God and couldn't be taken by others.[5]

---

5 Sheridan Voysey, "Terry Waite: Faith Held Hostage," interview for Hope 103.2, April 14, 2013.

David may have gone further and recognized that not only his soul but his whole life was in God's hands. But this did not make him passive—remember how he tricked Achish into releasing him? It did give him confidence to rest in God's sovereign grip of grace.

The second source of confidence is that David knows that he is on God's heart:

> Record my misery;
>> list my tears on your scroll—
>> are they not in your record?
> Then my enemies will turn back
>> when I call for help.
> By this I will know that God is for me. (56:8–9)

David asks God to record his tears. The Hebrew here is difficult to translate. It may mean, "Write my tears in your book of remembrance," or "Collect my tears in your bottle." In either case, it is an appeal to God's tenderhearted kindness.

Our tears are private and personal. We have seen how they are often the most powerful expression of our most profound grief. And our lives are often soaked in tears. Pastor and author Colin Smith describes them as "the shuddering of the body at the pain of the soul."[6]

God knows exactly what causes the pain and provokes our tears. They are recorded and remembered by him. So when

6   Colin S. Smith, *For All Who Grieve* (Louisville, KY: 10Publishing, 2020), 25.

we lament, we do not stand alone: God knows, and God cares. And, of course, in the incarnation of the Son of God, we find the greatest comfort of all. Jesus knows what it is to be hungry and thirsty; to rejoice at a wedding and to weep at a funeral; to be deserted and denied; to be beaten, mocked, abused, and tortured to death. Our grief may be caused by loneliness or bereavement or disappointment or betrayal. Jesus knows these too by personal experience, and this Friend will stay close to us when we grieve:

> Can we find a friend so faithful
> Who will all our sorrows share?
> Jesus knows our every weakness,
> Take it to the Lord in prayer.[7]

Psalm 56 ends on a note of great confidence:

> I am under vows to you, my God;
>   I will present my thank offerings to you.
> For you have delivered me from death
>   and my feet from stumbling,
> that I may walk before God
>   in the light of life. (56:12–13)

David promises that he will not forget how God has rescued him, but will present a thanksgiving offering at the first opportunity. He speaks of his deliverance as a past achievement—a done

---

7 Joseph Medlicott Scriven, "What a Friend We Have in Jesus," 1855.

deal. This may be a postscript written later than the rest of the psalm, but more likely it is an example of the "prophetic perfect," which means that David is writing about a future event of which he so certain that he can write as if it were already accomplished. David knew that God had promised to make him king (1 Sam. 16:12–13), so he could be confident that he would not die in Gath. We don't have this direct assurance of deliverance from danger or death, but God has promised us the ultimate deliverance from the grave, as sealed by the resurrection of Christ.

So a lamentation which began in the darkness ends with David walking before God in light and life.

Learning life lessons in trust

Reflecting on David's experience as outlined in Psalm 56, it seems to me that there are at least three helpful lessons for us today. We might describe them as the blessings which come from loss when we respond with godly lamentation.

Lesson 1: Loss drives us into the arms of God

David runs to God because he has nowhere else to go. He is at the end of his human resources, and his life hangs in the balance. When we are in distress, we lament because we have a relationship with God—and lamenting is a proof of this relationship.

The supreme purpose of our lives is to know God. We were created to glorify God and to enjoy him forever. In the beginning, Adam and Eve walked with God in the garden (Gen. 3:8), and one day we are destined to see him face to face (Rev. 22:4). Knowing God is the essence of salvation (John 17:3) and ought to be the supreme ambition of our lives:

> I want to know Christ—yes, to know the power of his resurrection and participation in his sufferings, becoming like him in his death, and so, somehow, attaining to the resurrection from the dead. (Phil. 3:10–11)

Of course, knowing God in Christ is often accomplished through pain and tears, and lamenting can be a pathway to a deeper intimacy with God. After his suffering, Job could confess, "My ears had heard of you but now my eyes have seen you" (Job 42:5).

And Elisabeth Elliot, whom I quoted earlier, wrote,

> I am not a theologian or a scholar, but I am very aware of the fact that pain is necessary to all of us. In my own life, I think I can honestly say that out of the deepest pain has come the strongest conviction of the presence of God and the love of God.[8]

God often leads us on a hard road so that, through a thousand intimacies along the way, we grow in our knowledge of his goodness and grace. He does not promise to save us from the furnace, but he promises to stand with us in the flames (Isa. 43:1–5).

---

8   As quoted in Brian Petree, *Help Me Help You: Get Your Mind Right* (Bloomington, IN: Westbow, 2020), 172.

Lesson 2: Loss tests our priorities

An idol is something or someone we trust to bring us satisfaction, and to which we turn for shelter when we are in trouble. We all face the danger of idolatry: the heart is an "idol factory,"[9] according to one well-known theologian, and it is constantly under siege (Ezek. 14:3).

When we think of idols, we usually think about sinful, forbidden pleasures which must be resisted. However, for most of us, the idols gripping our hearts are perfectly legitimate things which take the place of God. One of the greatest temptations we fall for in the life of faith is to enjoy God's gifts and to forget the Giver.

Grief strips away the idols that we love more than God. It changes our priorities and our attitudes towards the good things in our lives. It prunes us so that we will bear more fruit (John 15:1–5).

While in Gath, David was stripped of all his earthly comforts. Alone and surrounded by enemies, he has lost his home and his wife. He is a refugee whose situation is so precarious that he has to hide in the most perilous place possible, and his feigned insanity symbolises the depths to which he has sunk! Every idol—success, fame, position, human dignity, even—has been taken away.

So how does David respond? With honesty and integrity, he makes a choice. He will tell God how he feels, but he will also trust and rejoice insofar as men can take everything else from

---

9   John Calvin, *Institutes* I.11.8.

him, but not the Lord's presence. On another occasion when David has lost most of his earthly comforts, he writes,

> My heart says of you, "Seek his face!"
>   Your face, Lord, I will seek.
> I remain confident of this:
>   I will see the goodness of the Lord
>   in the land of the living.
> Wait for the Lord;
>   be strong and take heart
>   and wait for the Lord. (Ps. 27:8, 13–14)

As a teenager, I heard Richard Wurmbrand preach. He had been released from prison after fourteen years of being "tortured for Christ"[10] in communist Romania. His crime was that he refused to stop preaching Christ. I paraphrase from memory, but he spoke words to this effect:

> There were times when I sat alone in my cell—hungry, cold, and in pain from the latest beating. And as I sat there in the dark, I would sing songs of joy. They can take away my freedom and my comforts; they can rob me of my health and dignity; they can strip me of everyone I love; they can even take away my life. But they cannot take from me the firm grip of the nail-pierced hands of my Saviour.

---

10 The title of one of his books. See Voice of the Martyrs' *Wurmbrand: Tortured for Christ* (Colorado Springs, CO: David C. Cook Publications, 2018).

They cannot take my God away from me.

There is nothing wrong with any of the things which Wurmbrand lists. They are good gifts from a generous God, and it would be churlish to refuse to enjoy them (James 1:17). So we should savour what God sends without feeling guilty or being paralysed by the fear of losing it (Eccl. 2:24; 3:12–13).

It would also be wrong to suggest that God constantly removes these things because we are in danger of loving them too much. Moreover, it would be simply cruel and untrue to imply such a thing to a grieving person.

However, loss does remind us that we are pilgrims here, and that every joy and every sorrow is temporary. We must learn to hold things lightly. Life is about giving things back. So we should learn to rejoice in what we have rather than grieving unduly over what we have lost. And most of all, like David, we should glory in God—the treasure which we can never lose. Like Paul, we learn to say,

I know what it is to be in need, and I know what it is to have plenty. I have learned the secret of being content in any and every situation, whether well fed or hungry, whether living in plenty or in want. I can do all this through him who gives me strength. (Phil. 4:12–13)

Lesson 3: Loss makes our faith more vital

In extreme adversity, David found his faith stretched to the limits. However, his honest confession of need led to a humble confidence in God's promises. We saw earlier that his faith involved a deliberate decision to believe God's Word. Twice he tells us that this is the source of his faith: "In God, whose word I praise, in the LORD, whose word I praise" (Ps. 56:10).

It was the loss of earthly comforts that forced David to exercise this faith. Grief too strips away our self-confidence and forces us to rely on God. In the New Testament, Paul shared a similar experience:

> We do not want you to be uninformed, brothers and sisters, about the troubles we experienced in the province of Asia. We were under great pressure, far beyond our ability to endure, so that we despaired of life itself. Indeed, we felt we had received the sentence of death. But this happened that we might not rely on ourselves but on God, who raises the dead. He has delivered us from such a deadly peril, and he will deliver us again. (2 Cor. 1:8–10)

The pressure was overwhelming, but it forced the apostle to rely on God and not on his own resources.

Our faith grows with our trials, like a muscle which needs to be exercised. If I strap my arm to my chest for a year and then unstrap it, the muscles will have wasted, and it will be useless. It is a matter of "use it or lose it." And the same is true of faith. God often puts us in adverse circumstances in order to give us a spiritual workout. Paul had confidence for the future because his faith had been tested and tempered. He knew that God would deliver from future trials because of what he had done in the past—past grace being a token of future grace. As Paul expresses it elsewhere,

> We … glory in our sufferings, because we know that suffering produces perseverance; perseverance, character; and character, hope. (Rom. 5:3–4)

Self-reliance is the enemy of faith. By contrast, loss forces us to rely on God, not ourselves. It transforms our attitude towards ourselves, humbling us and removing our pride, and teaching us how fragile we really are.

We never really know that God is all we need until God is all that we have got.

Questions

1. "We know that we are not in control of our lives. Like Job, we cannot protect our possessions, family, and health from the uncertainties of life. We are all vulnerable, and our fear has an active imagination." Why do we want to be in control? Where do you feel vulnerable at the moment? In what ways does fear have an active imagination?

2. Read Psalm 139:1–6. What does God know about your circumstances? What is the point of telling him what he already knows?

3. Why do we need to preach to ourselves? What are the truths or messages you most often need to hear?

4. Read 2 Corinthians 12:7–10. The thorn that Paul refers to was a painful, chronic, limiting, and humiliating problem.

But how did it deepen Paul's relationship with God?

5. "Loss forces us to rely on God, not ourselves. It transforms our attitude to ourselves … ." How does this happen? How have you seen this happen in others' lives, or your own?

6

Learning Brokenness

It was on a sunny day at the beginning of the school holidays that my sister rang to tell me Mum had died.

I had gone into town to stock up on treats for five of our grandchildren who were coming to stay with us. We were bracing ourselves for this delightful invasion when the phone rang.

Mum died early on during the COVID-19 pandemic. She was in her nineties and had been frail for several months. We will never know whether or not she was one of the many victims of the virus which affected all our lives. But in some ways, death was a relief for Mum. She had lived through the war years and struggled with cancer, diabetes, heart disease, and dementia. I can count on the fingers of one hand the number of times she told me that she loved me, but I never doubted it for one minute. Kindness and generosity were her love languages, and these she spoke eloquently.

The funeral was a very subdued affair, respecting the COVID rules at the time. Only immediate family members gathered to reflect on her long life of selflessness. My kids cherished their "nanny" and wanted to express their love for her. For my part, I rejoiced that Mum had come to faith in her eighties, and that death for her was a release from confusion and an entry into the presence of Christ.

So we shared memories. We did the tasks that follow a funeral service. And after a couple of days, my wife and I began our journey home.

And then it happened.

I was suddenly filled with an overwhelming sense of guilt. It arrived totally unbidden, and it felt very real.

True guilt and false guilt

Along with anger, guilt is one of the two most common emotions we feel as we grieve. Guilt is devious and crafty. It comes unbidden, and against all reasonable objections, it refuses to be easily dismissed. It often runs deep and is resistant to logical arguments.

How do we explain it? It may be a reaction to the sense of helplessness which we experience in the face of death. We could do nothing to prevent the death of the person we loved. In Mum's case, death was a release, but it still felt wrong—as all death feels wrong in a world which is not as God originally designed it. But rationalizing does not bring relief.

Guilt arrives as we begin to think back and imagine all the things we might have done differently. Our minds are dominated by thoughts of "What if …?" and "If only …?" In my case, I began to think, "Could I have been a better son?"

I had left home at eighteen and never really returned. I had tried to honour Mum, but surely I could have done better. On the other hand, life was so busy with family and church. Then my wife became ill, and that had a major impact on everything. But I could have been more thoughtful and attentive. In the final years, my sister Julie had cared for Mum with courage and compassion—she is the real hero in our family. She visited her in the care home every day. I, by contrast, lived farther away and was much less frequent in my visits. And sometimes, because Mum had dementia, she just seemed so distant, and I didn't know what to say. It is ironic—a preacher lives to talk, but I didn't know what to say to my own mum. Julie was brilliant, but I was tongue-tied.

Regrets are cruel taskmasters.

All these thoughts invaded my mind, and I felt crushed. They were a self-imposed burden, and I think I knew deep down that they did not necessarily correspond to the reality of my relationship with Mum. But still, they would not go away.

What are we to make of experiences like this?

No relationship is perfect. I often tell young couples as I prepare them for matrimony that a good marriage is the union of two good forgivers. We do let one another down, and we need honestly to address the things which we could have done differently. Sometimes there will be real guilt which needs to find forgiveness and, if possible, reconciliation. The problem, though, with the guilt associated with bereavement is that there is no possibility of reconciliation. What's more, there is also a false guilt which is not the product of genuinely sinful actions or attitudes, but the result of the tidal wave of emotions swamping us when we grieve. Grief may amplify true guilt and also awaken in us feelings of false guilt.

Since then, I have found a book by Colin Smith really helpful. Colin enables us to distinguish true and false guilt:

False guilt comes when you take responsibility for something God did not call you to do or for something that was not under your control.

True guilt comes when you shirk responsibility for something that God called you to do or when you do what He has commanded you not to do.[1]

He continues,

The answer to false guilt is the truth and the answer to true guilt is grace. Our Lord Jesus Christ is "full of grace and truth" (John 1:14), and this means that in him we have all we need for dealing with guilt, whether it is true or false.[2]

Looking back now, I know that I could have been a better son, and I regret mistakes that I made. But I loved my mum, and she knew it, and I know she loved me and delighted in our relationship, even if she didn't say so. Most of my feelings of guilt were not justified. It may take time, but the citadel of false guilt does yield to truth. It may help to share such feelings with someone

---

1 Colin Smith, *For All Who Grieve: Navigating the Valley of Sorrow and Loss* (Louisville, KY: 10Publishing, 2020), 61.

2 Smith, *For All Who Grieve*, 61.

you trust. This is all part of bearing one another's burdens (Gal. 6:2).

But what if the guilt *is* real?

The gravity of sin

David wrote Psalm 51 as he wrestled with the consequences of real guilt. The inscription at the beginning tells us that it was "A psalm of David. When the prophet Nathan came to him after David had committed adultery with Bathsheba."

The story of David's sin with Bathsheba is well-known and does not need to be rehearsed here.[3] Instead of leading his people to war, as a warrior-king should do, David stays in Jerusalem and falls into sin. As C. S. Lewis wisely put it,

> The long, dull, monotonous years of middle-aged prosperity or middle-aged adversity are excellent campaigning weather for the devil.[4]

David gave in to lust and committed adultery. Fearing the consequences of his actions, he practiced deceit and orchestrated murder. There is a gravity about sin, and once we surrender to it, we cannot control the consequences. Yet no one challenged him, and life remained as it always was. So David got away with it.

But, of course, he didn't.

The chapter which describes David's descent does not

---

3 See 2 Samuel 11–12.

4 C. S. Lewis, *The Screwtape Letters* (London: Collins/Fontana, 1955), 110.

mention God—he is all but absent. Except that in the final verse we read the sobering words: "But the thing David had done displeased the LORD" (2 Sam. 11:27).

God knew, and David knew. In another psalm which may refer to the same situation, David describes the inner turmoil that sin brings when we try to ignore God and supress our consciences:

> When I kept silent,
>   my bones wasted away
>   through my groaning all day long.
> For day and night
>   your hand was heavy on me;
> my strength was sapped
>   as in the heat of summer. (Ps. 32:3–4)

God sent the prophet Nathan to confront David, and he was broken by God's word. He confessed his sin, and God declared his judgement:

> Then David said to Nathan, "I have sinned against the LORD."
>   Nathan replied, "The LORD has taken away your sin. You are not going to die. But because by doing this you have shown utter contempt for the LORD, the son born to you will die." (2 Sam. 12:13–14)

Brokenness and lament

In this context, David wrote Psalm 51 to express the depths of his brokenness before God, in what is usually described as a "penitential psalm."[5] However, we could also classify this as a psalm of lament, although most of David's psalms of lament occur when he is the victim of sin. Here he is the *perpetrator* of sin, lamenting the depths of sin in his own life, which comes from the bleakest self-knowledge:

> For I know my transgressions,
>   and my sin is always before me. …
> Surely I was sinful at birth,
>   sinful from the time my mother conceived me. (vv. 3, 5)

This is a cry from the heart for the forgiveness which only God can give. David does not try to bargain with God—he has nothing to bargain with. He simply casts himself on God's grace:

> Have mercy on me, O God,
>   according to your unfailing love;
> according to your great compassion
>   blot out my transgressions.
> Wash away all my iniquity
>   and cleanse me from my sin. (vv. 1–2)

Cleanse me with hyssop, and I will be clean;

---

5   There are seven penitential psalms: Psalm 6, 32, 38, 51, 102, 130, and 143.

wash me, and I will be whiter than snow. (v. 7)

Hide your face from my sins
    and blot out all my iniquity. (v. 9)

Deliver me from the guilt of bloodshed, O God,
    you who are God my Savior (v. 14)

David knows what he has lost and is afraid he may lose even more:

Let me hear joy and gladness;
    let the bones you have crushed rejoice. (v. 8)

Do not cast me from your presence
    or take your Holy Spirit from me.
Restore to me the joy of your salvation
    and grant me a willing spirit, to sustain me. (vv. 11–12)

David does not dismiss the whole sacrificial system (vv. 18–19), but he has come to see that it is the broken heart of the penitent sinner which truly delights God:

You do not delight in sacrifice, or I would bring it;
    you do not take pleasure in burnt offerings.
My sacrifice, O God, is a broken spirit;
    a broken and contrite heart
    you, God, will not despise. (vv. 16–17)

Beyond this, David is conscious that sin is not merely an aberration, but that it flows from a heart which is deceitful and needs to be renewed (compare Jer. 17:9):

> Create in me a pure heart, O God,
>   and renew a steadfast spirit within me. (v. 10)

With this full forgiveness and this renewed heart, David will serve God, warning others and worshipping God for his amazing grace:

> Then I will teach transgressors your ways,
>   so that sinners will turn back to you. …
> Open my lips, Lord,
>   and my mouth will declare your praise. (vv. 13, 15)

Embracing brokenness

But isn't all this talk of penitence and brokenness all very Old-Covenant and pre-Jesus? Or doesn't it smack of some kind of medieval self-flagellation? Surely the gospel means that when we are forgiven, we can forget our past failures and now bask in the warm glow of God's grace? By harping on about sin, aren't we demeaning forgiveness? God is our kind and generous heavenly Father—does he really want us to wallow in guilt and experience brokenness?

Let's look at this under three headings.

Forgiven and cleansed

Firstly, it is true that the heart of the gospel is forgiveness. At the cross, God deals with both our guilt and our shame. He does not want us to wallow in our sin. We have been reconciled to our Father in heaven, and when he sees us, he sees the impeccable robes of Christ's righteousness. David knew this forgiveness and would later write,

> Blessed is the one
>> whose transgressions are forgiven,
>> whose sins are covered.
> Blessed is the one
>> whose sin the LORD does not count against them
>> and in whose spirit is no deceit. (Ps. 32:1–2)

When he recounts all the ways that God has blessed him, forgiveness is first on David's list (Ps. 103:1–5). It is the same message found in the New Testament:

> If we confess our sins, he is faithful and just to forgive us our sins and purify us from all unrighteousness. (1 John 1:9)

There is no room for unhealthy introspection and wallowing here!

Ongoing repentance

Secondly, we have an ongoing sin problem even after we have

become Christians. Surrounding the passage in which John assures us of the forgiveness of sin, he warns us,

> If we claim to be without sin, we deceive ourselves and the truth is not in us. … If we claim we have not sinned, we make him out to be a liar and his word is not in us. (1 John 1:8, 10)

Jesus knew this, and he encouraged us to pray not only for daily bread but also, by implication, for daily forgiveness (Matt. 6:11–12).

Commentators disagree on the correct interpretation of Romans 7, but it does seem to describe Paul's ongoing conflict with the corruption of his own heart:

> So I find this law at work: Although I want to do good, evil is right there with me. For in my inner being I delight in God's law; but I see another law at work in me, waging war against the law of my mind and making me a prisoner of the law of sin at work within me. (vv. 21–23)

This is my ongoing personal experience too. In my thirties I naively thought that by the time I hit my sixties, the battle with the old nature would be won. It isn't! I need the grace of repentance every day. The old nature may be dead, but it won't lie down. I am now convinced that sin will be nipping at my heels until the end of the journey.

It is no wonder that the first of Martin Luther's ninety-five theses states:

> When our Lord and Master Jesus Christ said, "Repent" (Mt 4:17), he willed the entire life of believers to be one of repentance.[6]

New Testament truth too

Thirdly, the call for brokenness in the face of sin is not confined to the Old Testament. Jesus commends the brokenness of the sinful woman who

> stood behind him at his feet weeping, [and] began to wet his feet with her tears. Then she wiped them with her hair, kissed them and poured perfume on them. (Luke 7:38)[7]

James writes,

> Come near to God and he will come near to you. Wash your hands, you sinners, and purify your hearts, you double-minded. Grieve, mourn and wail. Change your laughter to mourning and your joy to gloom. (4:8–9)

This broken and humble spirit is at the heart of the beatitudes (Matt. 5:3–10). The second one reads, "Blessed are those who mourn, for they will be comforted" (v. 4).

---

6   For more on the Luther's *Theses*, including their full text, see Stephen Nichols, ed., *Martin Luther's Ninety-Five Theses* (Phillipsburg, NJ: P&R Publishing, 2022).

7   See Luke 7:36–50.

We often take this to apply to the grief which comes through the loss of a loved one. Now, I don't think that this is an illegitimate application, but the context suggests something else. John Stott comments,

> It is plain from the context that those here promised comfort are not primarily those who mourn the loss of a loved one, but those who mourn the loss of their innocence, their righteousness, their self-respect. It is not the sorrow of bereavement to which Christ refers, but the sorrow of repentance.[8]

Martyn Lloyd-Jones puts it like this:

> To mourn is something that follows of necessity from being "poor in spirit." It is quite inevitable. As I confront God and His holiness and contemplate the life that I am meant to live, I see myself, my utter helplessness and hopelessness. I discover my quality of spirit and immediately that makes me mourn. I must mourn about the fact that I am like that.[9]

Confession leads to contrition, which involves sorrow and remorse for sin. Paul describes this "godly sorrow" in 2 Corinthians 7 as follows:

---

8   John Stott, *The Message of the Sermon on the Mount* (London: Inter-Varsity Press, 1978) 40–41.

9   Martyn Lloyd-Jones, *Sermon on the Mount* (London: Inter-Varsity Press, 1977), 58.

Godly sorrow brings repentance that leads to salvation and leaves no regret, but worldly sorrow brings death. See what this godly sorrow has produced in you: what earnestness, what eagerness to clear yourselves, what indignation, what alarm, what longing, what concern, what readiness to see justice done. At every point you have proved yourselves to be innocent in this matter. (vv. 10–11)

Lamenting over sin does not involve a theatrical wailing or a beating of the breast. It does not have to be showy to be authentic. Nor is it a form of self-justification. We do not gain any merit or favour with God because of our acts of contrition. Nonetheless, it is real.

In our cultural context, this can seem jarring. In an age that may have re-discovered the glory of grace, the idea of lamenting over our sins seems like a step backwards. We can glory in the gospel of justification by faith alone, but at the same time we need a clear view of the horrors of sin and the need for brokenness in the face of our own rebellion against God. We believe in grace, but not in cheap grace.

We need to learn to lament for our sins.

We need to learn the grace of brokenness.

The blessings of brokenness

Returning to Psalm 51, we discover that David gives us a galaxy of reasons to embrace brokenness and to learn to lament for our sin.

Brokenness alerts us to the enormity of sin

David knew that his sin was against Bathsheba and Uriah her husband. He'd used his position to exploit his power and abuse Bathsheba. He then went even further and, shockingly, manipulated circumstances to murder Uriah. So his sin had dire consequences for the people involved. But in his brokenness, David came to see that at heart, his sin was an act of rebellion against God:[10]

> Against you, you only, have I sinned
>   and done what is evil in your sight;
> so you are right in your verdict
>   and justified when you judge. (Ps. 51:4)

There can be no small sin because there is no small God to sin against. Sin assaults God, while also assaulting human beings who have been made in his image. And its presence, pervasiveness, and destructive power wreak havoc in lives. But it is first and foremost an affront to God: it blasphemes him and seeks to pull him from his throne. John Bunyan described sin as

> the dare of [God's] justice, the rape of his mercy, the jeer of his patience, the slight of his power, the contempt of his love! It is the fist that strikes the face of Christ.[11]

10 See also 2 Samuel 12:13.

11 John Bunyan, "Mr. John Bunyan's Dying Sayings," *The Pilgrim's Progress and Other Works by John Bunyan*, ed. George Offor (Glasgow: William Mackenzie, 1861), 786.

When the soldiers had covered Jesus' eyes, they came and smashed him in the face, demanding that he identify who hit him (Luke 22:64). Our sin is like this fist striking Jesus' face.

Sin is not just the transgression of a legal code; it is the fracturing of a precious and intimate familial bond. It is the arrogant and high-handed rejection of the goodness which the Father provides and offers. More fundamentally, it is the rejection of the Father himself.

Sin is contrary to the purpose and will of God. It is the desire to be other than God has created us to be (Gen. 3:5, 22); it opposes itself to everything that God wills and commands. Sin is contrary to God's nature, for he is absolutely holy and must hate sin (1 John 1:5–6).

And for Christians, sinning is against the One who loved us and gave himself up for us (Eph. 5:2). Sin is always personal, but when we sin, it is not only an insult against majesty—it is a ferocious violation of love. David had experienced countless blessings from the Lord. He had been ransomed, healed, restored, and forgiven.[12] So his failure was immeasurable ingratitude in the face immeasurable grace. Or think how Luke describes Peter's denial of Jesus:

The Lord turned and looked straight at Peter. Then Peter remembered the word the Lord had spoken to him: "Before the rooster crows today, you will disown me three

---

12   See Henry Lyte, "Praise, My Soul, the King of Heaven," 1834.

times." And he went outside and wept bitterly. (Luke 22:61–62)

What pain was in that look! What anguish was in Peter's heart! A broken man, he weeps for his failure to love Jesus … All my sins too are failures to the One who has never failed me. And they are not infrequent either.

Brokenness is both the proper response to sin and the reminder of its enormity.

Brokenness helps us resist sin

We have to battle against sin every day. So we need as much ammunition as we can muster to resist its persistent pull. One of the advantages of brokenness is that it reminds us of the horrendous consequences of sin.

David describes these consequences in Psalm 51. Notice the number of times that he pleads for cleansing:

> Blot out my transgressions.
> Wash away all my iniquity
>   and cleanse me from my sin. (vv. 1–2)

> Cleanse me with hyssop, and I will be clean;
>   wash me, and I will be whiter than snow. (v. 7)

> Hide your face from my sins
>   and blot out all my iniquity. (v. 9)

David knows all too well that sin leaves a stain. It makes us feel dirty; we know that we have lost our innocence. Yes, we can be forgiven and reconciled to God, but we can never regain our innocence. More than that, sin creates memories that are difficult to erase: "For I know my transgressions, and my sin is always before me" (v. 3).

We often say that there is no forgiveness without forgetfulness, but this is simply not true. Sin often leaves scar tissue which no cosmetic can hide, as Lady Macbeth discovered when she could not remove the stain of blood from her hands:

Here's the smell of the blood still; all the perfumes of Arabia will not sweeten this little hand.[13]

David experienced forgiveness, but his sin unleashed violence and murder which would affect his own family:

Why did you despise the word of the LORD by doing what is evil in his eyes? You struck down Uriah the Hittite with the sword and took his wife to be your own. You killed him with the sword of the Ammonites. Now, therefore, the sword will never depart from your house, because you despised me and took the wife of Uriah the Hittite to be your own. (2 Sam. 12:9–10)

Read 2 Samuel 13 and the following chapters, and you will see

13 William Shakespeare, *Macbeth*, 5.1.20.

how this played out.

Brokenness has a way of humbling our hearts and causing us to hate sin and its consequences. It steels our nerve to resist temptation, or, to change the metaphor, you are much less likely to play with fire when you have been scorched by its heat. It makes us aware of the bankruptcy of our own resources and causes us to cast ourselves on Christ.

Listen to Puritan preacher Thomas Brooks:

Faith puts the soul upon grieving for sin, upon combating with sin, upon weeping over sin, upon trembling at the occasions of sin, upon resisting temptations that lead to sin, upon fighting it out to the death with sin.[14]

Brokenness is the gateway to worship

There is no joy without brokenness. Read through the psalms, and you will see that David was a man who enjoyed God. The Lord was his rock and fortress (Pss. 18:2; 31:2,3; 62:2, 6); his shepherd (Psalm 23); his light and salvation (Ps. 27:1; 68:20); his strength and shield (Pss. 18:2; 28:7; 59:11). In a time of great danger, David is clear about his priorities:

One thing I ask from the LORD,
    this only do I seek:
that I may dwell in the house of the LORD

14 Thomas Brooks, *Heaven on Earth: A Treatise on Christian Assurance*, The Complete Works of Thomas Brooks, vol. 2 (Edinburgh: James Nichol, 1866), 451.

all the days of my life,
to gaze on the beauty of the Lord
and to seek him in his temple. (Ps. 27:4)

For David, the greatest horror was to lose the smile of God. What did the kingdom mean without fellowship with the King of Glory? We can pretend that things are well with us while we are in a backslidden state, but in our hearts we know that we no longer delight in God or enjoy the blessings of salvation.

David had lost joy and gladness and longed for their return (51:8, 12). His greatest fear was that he would be cast away from God forever (51:11). The road to restoration is the road of brokenness: "My sacrifice, O God, is a broken spirit; a broken and contrite heart you, God, will not despise" (51:17). Elsewhere David says, "The Lord is close to the brokenhearted and saves those who are crushed in spirit" (Ps. 34:18).

And Isaiah knew this too:

For this is what the high and exalted One says—
he who lives forever, whose name is holy:
"I live in a high and holy place,
but also with the one who is contrite and lowly in spirit,
to revive the spirit of the lowly
and to revive the heart of the contrite." (Isa. 57:15)

And

These are the ones I look on with favor:

> those who are humble and contrite in spirit,
> and who tremble at my word. (Isa. 66:2)

Brokenness leads to real joy, authentic worship (51:15), and genuine witness (51:13). When our broken hearts yield to God, we rediscover his grace, as we did when we first believed. We can sing with Charles Wesley, "And can it be that I should gain an interest in the Saviour's blood?"

Brokenness is not wasted. Listen to another Puritan, Richard Sibbes:

When a man sets himself apart to weep over Christ and sees his sins for the dishonour that is offered to God's name, and that his mourning is holy and spiritual mourning, he shall never have cause to repent of this time that is so spent, although he have spent many days and hours in that action.[15]

Brokenness truly is the gateway to blessing. And all of this blessing has been won for us by Jesus Christ.

It is to him that we will next turn our attention.

Questions

1. How can we distinguish between true guilt and false guilt? What is an appropriate response to each?

---

15 Richard Sibbes, *Spiritual Mourning*, The Complete Works of Richard Sibbes, D.D., vol. 6, ed. Alexander Balloch Grosart (Edinburgh: James Nichol, 1863), 270.

2. Read Exodus 20:1–17 and 2 Samuel 11–12. Which commandments did David break? Now read 2 Samuel 13. How were David's sins repeated by his sons?

3. Psalm 32 may well have been written sometime after Psalm 51. What had David learned by the time he wrote this psalm?

4. For the Christian, sin is immeasurable failure in the face of immeasurable grace. How should this reality affect the way we think about sin?

5. Read Psalm 51 again. Make a list of David's prayers. What marks of authentic brokenness do you find in this psalm?

7

Learning from the Darkness and from Jesus

Sometimes there seems to be no light at the end of the tunnel.

The psalms of lament are painful to read, but they describe a journey into the light. Having turned to God, the psalmist moves from complaint through prayer to trust. Darkness is dispelled, and hope is kindled. But not in Psalm 88, which stands alone among the psalms of lament. In commentator Derek Kidner's estimation, there is "no sadder prayer in the Psalter."[1]

The psalmist, Heman the Ezrahite,[2] cries out to God and brings his complaints to the Almighty. His psalm is one long desperate cry: "I cry out before you … I call out … I cry to you …." Death seems immanent, his anguish is overwhelming, and he feels totally alone and abandoned to the darkness: "You have

---

1   Derek Kidner, *Psalms 73–150: A Commentary on Books III–V of the Psalms* (Downers Grove, IL: InterVarsity Press, 1973), 316.

2   Heman was a Levite and the grandson of Samuel (see 1 Chron. 6:33, 15:17). He was identified as one of three musicians appointed by King David "for the ministry of prophesying, accompanied by harps, lyres and cymbals" (1 Chron. 25:1). He had a reputation for wisdom (1 Kings 4:31).

taken from me friend and neighbor—darkness is my closest friend" (88:18).

In Hebrew, "darkness" is the last word of the psalm. One is reminded of Simon & Garfunkel's "The Sound of Silence."[3] Deserted by even his closest friends, who are repulsed when they look at him (v. 8), the psalmist feels that the only friend left to him is the darkness. In his despair, he is thinking about the darkness of death:

> I am overwhelmed with troubles
>   and my life draws near to death.
> I am counted among those who go down to the pit.
> (vv. 3–4)

> You have put me in the lowest pit,
>   in the darkest depths. (v. 6)

> From my youth I have suffered and been close to death;
>   I have borne your terrors and am in despair. (v. 15)

We do not know his circumstances, but the psalmist feels that they are not accidental—he is suffering at the hands of God: "Your wrath lies heavily on me; you have overwhelmed me with all your waves." (v. 7)

Here is the voice of despair, anguish, and darkest misery. It is

---

3   Written by Paul Simon over several months in 1963 and 1964.

"winter but never Christmas."[4]

He bombards heaven with his questions:

> Do you show your wonders to the dead?
>> Do their spirits rise up and praise you? (v. 10)

> Why, LORD, do you reject me
>> and hide your face from me? (v. 14)

But God is silent. The heavens remain as brass. Yet Heman knows God and has experienced his salvation in the past:

> LORD, you are the God who saves me;
>> day and night I cry out to you.
> May my prayer come before you;
>> turn your ear to my cry. (vv. 1–2)

> I call to you, LORD, every day;
>> I spread out my hands to you. (v. 9)

> But I cry to you for help, LORD;
>> in the morning my prayer comes before you. (v. 13)

But now, it seems, God has turned away. He is there, but he is silent. God does not care—for if he did, surely he would act.

---

4 This quote from C. S. Lewis's *The Lion, the Witch, and the Wardrobe* describes life in Narnia before the coming of Aslan, Lewis's great Christ figure. The first sign that he is coming is the arrival of Father Christmas!

The psalmist feels ignored, discounted, snubbed, rebuffed, and rejected. That is no way to treat your friends!

No hope?

Can we find any hope in this psalm?

First, the psalm bears testimony to the fact that sometimes God's people do indeed experience deep distress. And the darkness can stretch on for a long time. We often feel that dire circumstances are evidence that somehow we have been abandoned by God. And there is a line of teaching which insists that Christians should never suffer or experience pain of any sort: God wants you to be healthy, wealthy, and happy. If you are not, then it is your fault—either because of the absence of faith or the presence of sin. (We reflected on this earlier.)

But this view is not true to experience, and more importantly, it is not true to Scripture, as Psalm 88 bears witness:

In this psalm, Heman makes a map of his life's history, he puts down all the dark places through which he has travelled. He mentions his sins, his sorrows, his hopes (if he had any), his fears, his woes, and so on. Now, that is real prayer, laying your case before the Lord.[5]

The Bible is realistic about suffering, reminding us that unrelieved pain may well be our earthly lot. The laments usually end

---

5 Charles Spurgeon, "Heman's Sorrowful Psalm," sermon preached September 25, 1887, and published in *The Metropolitan Tabernacle Pulpit*, vol. 41 (Edinburgh: Banner of Truth, 1969), 469–480.

with hope, but a happy ending is a bonus, not a due. We follow a crucified Saviour who was utterly perfect and yet he experienced unimaginable grief and pain. Is the servant above the master?

The second thing to notice is that Psalm 88 is actually in the Bible! It was God who placed this anguished psalm in the Psalter. So what does this mean? It doesn't mean that the fears of the psalmist are justified: he feels abandoned by God, but this is not true, for even in our darkest hours, God has not forsaken us. But the fact that the Holy Spirit caused this lament to be penned surely means that God encourages his people to be honest about their deepest anxieties and fears.

Psalm 88 reinforces the invitation to honesty we noted earlier. Indeed, there are times when Heman's words are bold and even disrespectful. We are reminded here of some of Job's complaints. Yet the inclusion of the psalm does not encourage impudence.

The Lord is tender towards his people, and as David recognises in Psalm 103:

> As a father has compassion on his children,
>   so the LORD has compassion on those who fear him;
> for he knows how we are formed,
>   he remembers that we are dust.
> The life of mortals is like grass. (vv. 13–15)

The presence of this psalm in inspired Scripture shows that God knows how people feel when they are desperate, and he does not reject them in their despair. Rather than abandoning them, he identifies with them and invites them to pour out their hearts to him.

Thirdly, the psalm is not a rejection of God, but an anguished cry to him. However dark our circumstances, we can always run into his arms—even when we do not feel their warm embrace. Heman begins by calling God his Saviour and addressing his complaints to someone he knows:

> Lord, you are the God who saves me;
>   day and night I cry out to you.
> May my prayer come before you;
>   turn your ear to my cry. (vv. 1–2)

Bad as things are, he has experienced God's salvation in the past, and past grace, as noted earlier, is a token of future grace. Heman is confused, but he is not bitter. This glimmer of light in the darkness shows that even on the threshold of death, he has not abandoned hope. All his comforts have vanished, and yet he will not let go of God. In his weakness, he holds on to the One who can turn darkness into light.

In this sense, the psalm is not evidence of a lack of faith, but rather a demonstration of remarkable trust amid impossible circumstances. There is never a time to stop praying, even when our prayers seem too feeble and powerless.

According to Derek Kidner,

This author, like Job, does not give up. He completes his prayer, still in the dark and totally unrewarded. The taunt, "Does Job fear God for naught?", is answered yet again.

Like Job, the author has received no satisfactory answer for why his life has turned out as miserably as it has. But also, like Job, he does not "curse God and die" (Job 2:9). Rather, he is seen clinging to God.[6]

Fourthly and finally, we can be fairly certain that God did bring the psalmist out of the darkness. How do we know this? The title of the psalm gives us hope. The author was among those who established the singing guilds set up by David to lead worship. Known as the Kohathite, these men pioneered liturgical worship and composed several psalms which would come to be used in the temple (Pss. 42–49; 84–85; 87–88).

We do not know when Heman wrote this psalm, but the fact that he went on to lead the Kohathite guilds (1 Chron. 6:33, 37) suggests that he did eventually find light amid his darkness. The Lord had not abandoned him. Indeed, we might say that his experience of suffering tempered him and made him stronger, for we learn more about God in the darkness than in the light.

There is a wonderful moment in J. R. R. Tolkien's epic *The Lord of the Rings*. Sam, who turns out to be one of the most unexpected heroes, faces what looks like the certainty of death. Tolkien writes,

But even as hope died in Sam, or seemed to die, it was turned to new strength. Sam's plain hobbit-face grew

---

6   Kidner, *Psalms 73–150*, 319, as quoted in Ligon Duncan, *When Pain Is Real and God Seems Silent: Finding Hope in the Psalms* (Wheaton, IL: Crossway, 2020), 26.

stern, almost grim, as the will hardened in him, and he felt through all his limbs a thrill, as if he was turning into some creature of stone and steel that neither despair nor weariness nor endless barren miles could subdue.[7]

When you have walked the valley of the shadow of death with your Shepherd, even though you may not have felt his presence, you are stronger and more resilient. You can speak of God with a more authentic confidence than ever before. Heman came to see that "his existence was no mistake; there was a divine plan bigger than he knew, and a place in it is reserved most carefully for him."[8]

Thousands of years later, we can be grateful that Heman wrote this psalm, because it brings light to our wounded souls when we feel as if we are in the darkness.

Behold the Man

But beyond all this, there is another level at which we can read this psalm. Think again about its final words: "You have taken from me friend and neighbor—darkness is my closest friend" (v. 18).

The psalmist was experiencing outward or circumstantial darkness—he was alone and facing death. But he also felt as if he was being abandoned by God—an inner darkness of despair. Darkness is a better friend than a God who is no longer there.

7   J. R. R. Tolkien, *The Return of the King* (London: HarperCollins, 1967), 913.

8   Kidner, *Psalms 73–150*, 319.

The outer darkness of circumstances was real and undeniable. But the inner darkness of abandonment was an illusion: his fears were simply not true. We know that God never abandons his people, even when he feels a million miles away. The hopelessness experienced by the psalmist was not real. God had not turned his face away; he never does this with his children.

But there was a day when God did turn his face away, from his Son.

Fast-forward a thousand years to the place called Calvary. "From noon until three in the afternoon darkness came over all the land" (Matt. 27:45) For three hours, the cross was a busy and noisy place. People came and went. A few sympathized with Jesus, but most cursed him. Jesus prayed for his enemies. He reached out in love to his mother and his beloved disciple. He spoke words of grace to the dying thief. Then suddenly, at noon, when the sun is at its zenith, darkness fell over the land.

This was a supernatural darkness—a real and profound quenching of the light. How are we to explain it? Theologians have pondered its significance for millennia. Perhaps it was the response of nature to the death of Christ the Creator. The poet John Donne reflects this in one of his poems:

Who sees God's face, that is self-life, must die;
What a death were it then to see God die?
It made his own Lieutenant Nature shrink,
It made his footstool crack, and the Sun wink.
Could I behold those hands which span the Poles,

And tune all spheres at once pierced with those holes?[9]

But there is more to it than this. Darkness in the Bible is a symbol of judgement. The penultimate plague in Egypt was darkness over the land for three days (Exod. 10:21–29). This was followed by the death of the firstborn (Exod. 11:1–12:30). Darkness descends on Calvary for three hours, and then God's firstborn Son breathes his last. The prophet Amos reflects this theme of judgement when he speaks about the day of the Lord:

> Woe to you who long
>   for the day of the Lord!
> Why do you long for the day of the Lord?
>   That day will be darkness, not light. (Amos 5:18)

For Israel, this would be the darkness of exile. This was not an accident of history, but God drawing near to judge them for their sin:

> Therefore this is what I will do to you, Israel,
>   and because I will do this to you, Israel,
>   prepare to meet your God. (4:12)

And this brings us back to the cross. Out of that darkness came the most shocking cry of lament recorded in the Bible:

---

9   John Donne, "Good Friday, 1613. Riding Westward," lines 17–22, *The Complete English Poems*, ed. Robin Robbins, Longman Annotated English Poets (London: Longman, 2010), 562.

About three in the afternoon Jesus cried out in a loud voice, *"Eli, Eli, lema sabachthani?"* (which means "My God, my God, why have you forsaken me?"). (Matt. 27:46)

This abandonment and darkness were real. The darkness that Jesus experienced was literal. It also symbolised the profound pain that he was experiencing at that moment. But there was a deeper level on which Jesus was experiencing judgement as he became a sin offering. Heman only felt that he was forsaken; Jesus was truly forsaken.

How can we explain this?

In my place, condemned

To understand the darkness of Calvary, we need to understand the profound holiness of God and his absolute antipathy to sin. This hatred of unrighteousness is manifested in his wrath. Jim Packer explains it like this:

God's wrath in the Bible is never the capricious, self-indulgent, irritable, morally ignoble thing that human anger so often is. It is, instead, a right and necessary reaction to objective moral evil.[10]

New Testament scholar Leon Morris says,

---

10 J. I. Packer, *Knowing God*, 20th anniv. edition (Downers Grove, IL: InterVarsity, 1993), 151.

The biblical writers habitually use for the divine wrath a word [*orgē*] which denotes not so much a sudden flaring up of passion which is soon over, as a strong and settled opposition to all that is evil arising out of God's very nature.[11]

This explains the profundity of the sufferings of Christ. A few days before the cross, he spoke of it with dread:

The hour has come for the Son of Man to be glorified. … Now my soul is troubled, and what shall I say? "Father, save me from this hour"? No, it was for this very reason I came to this hour. Father, glorify your name! (John 12:23, 27–28)

For Jesus, the cross was a place of horror. His words give us a unique window into his soul: the word "troubled" carries the idea of being perplexed and agitated and amazed. It can be used of a tempestuous storm at sea when the waves rise and threaten to sink our poor, pathetic little boat. Light has gone, and deepest darkest surrounds us. *That* is the word Jesus uses to describe his inner turmoil. We are reminded of the garden of Gethsemane, where Jesus was also "sorrowful and troubled," confessing that his soul was "overwhelmed with sorrow to the point of death" (Matt. 26:37–38). There he pleaded for the cup of judgement to

---

11 Leon Morris, *The Apostolic Preaching of the Cross* (Grand Rapids: Eerdmans, 1956), 162–163.

be taken away (Mark 14:36), and he sweat great drops of blood (Luke 22:44).

What caused Jesus such horror? Crucifixion was ghastly, but it was more than that. Jesus died as a substitute and, in his death, satisfied the Father's just and holy wrath against our sin. Like a lightning conductor, he drew to himself the entire wrath that his people deserved. God treated his Son as if he were the worst sinner who'd ever lived. During the three hours of darkness, he who knew no sin was made sin for us (2 Cor. 5:21). During his earthly life, he had lived in the consciousness of God's smile. But as he bore our sins and faced his Father's wrath, that smile became a frown. This alone explains the horror of anticipation with which Jesus approaches the cross. It is a new experience for Christ. We may try to speculate on what it means, but we are confronted with mystery. Where our minds cannot journey, it is better for our knees to bow and our hearts humbly to acknowledge the wonder of God's love.

Comfort for us today

So how does this help us when we are in the darkness?

We see now that there is a huge difference between the darkness Heman described and the darkness Christ experienced. The latter was real and profound. And because Jesus tasted this darkness, we never will. He went into the darkness so that even if we feel alone and alienated from God, we can know that he is always with us. We lament within earshot of Calvary. As John Stott said,

The cross does not solve the problem of suffering—but it

supplies the essential perspective from which to look at it. I could never myself believe in God's love if it were not for the cross. The only God I believe in is the one Nietzsche ridiculed as the God on the cross.[12]

What is more, the fact that Jesus, the perfect man, lamented in the face of his suffering gives us permission to be human! He approached suffering with honesty and authenticity. He was not glib or casual about what he was about to face. He articulated his pain, and his Father heard his cries. Like Jesus, we can be honest with God.

The cross proves that God knows and cares for us when we are overwhelmed with sorrow. When we lament, it is easy to feel isolated from all human comfort. No one understands. We feel isolated and disorientated. Where is God? He feels like a distant deity—a kind of infinite iceberg.

But even in the Old Testament this view of God is challenged again and again. When the Lord calls Moses, he tells him of his deep concern for his people:

The LORD said, "I have indeed seen the misery of my people in Egypt. I have heard them crying out because of their slave drivers, and I am concerned about their suffering." (Exod. 3:7)

Years later, in the darkest hours of Israel's loss and lamentation,

12 John Stott, *Through the Bible Through the Year* (Oxford: Lion Hudson, 2006), 88.

Jeremiah is comforted by the memory of these truths:

> Because of the LORD's great love we are not consumed,
>   for his compassions never fail.
> They are new every morning;
>   great is your faithfulness. (Lam. 3:22–23)

But it is in the coming of Christ that God embraces our human fragility and stands with us in our vulnerability and lament. In Christ the eternal Word takes on flesh and dwells among us (John 1:1, 14). Jesus experienced thirst and weariness (John 4:6). He was moved by the infirmity of the shepherd-less people:

> When he saw the crowds, he had compassion for them, because they were harassed and helpless, like sheep without a shepherd. (Matt. 9:36)

Jesus was frequently moved with compassion—for someone suffering with leprosy (Mark 1:41); for the widow whose only son had died (Luke 7:13); for two blind men (Matt. 20:34). He invites us to find refuge in him:

> Come to me, all you who are weary and burdened, and I will give you rest. Take my yoke upon you and learn from me, for I am gentle and humble in heart, and you will find rest for your souls. For my yoke is easy and my burden is light. (Matt. 11:28–30)

When we lament, we do so with One who has experienced real grief that drove him to tears (Luke 19:41; Heb. 5:7–9). When we surrender to tears, we are in good company.

Openly and unapologetically, Jesus wept at the tomb of his friend. This proves that weeping itself is not a sign of weakness, for Jesus is the strong Son of God who can stand toe-to-toe with disorder or disease or demons or death itself and still emerge the conqueror.

Nor are tears a sign of unbelief, for Jesus was confident that he was going to raise Lazarus from the dead: "Our friend Lazarus has fallen asleep; but I am going there to wake him up" (John 11:11).

And Jesus had no doubts whatsoever about his own identity:

Jesus said to her, "I am the resurrection and the life. The one who believes in me will live, even though they die; and whoever lives by believing in me will never die. Do you believe this?" (vv. 25–26)

He prays with total assurance, and he issues commands with absolute confidence:

So they took away the stone. Then Jesus looked up and said, "Father, I thank you that you have heard me. I knew that you always hear me, but I said this for the benefit of the people standing here, that they may believe that you sent me."

When he had said this, Jesus called in a loud

voice, "Lazarus, come out!" The dead man came out, his hands and feet wrapped with strips of linen, and a cloth around his face. (vv. 41–44)

So weeping is certainly not a sign of unbelief or any lack of confidence!

Why, then, did Jesus weep? Jesus wept with the people he loved. He felt their pain, and it moved his heart. He experienced first-hand the pain which we know when loss invades our lives. And he stands with us in the solidarity of our suffering because he too wept for those he loved.

As Charles Spurgeon said,

There is infinitely more in these two words than any sermonizer, or student of the Word, will ever be able to bring out of them, even though he should apply the microscope of the most attentive consideration. "Jesus wept." Instructive fact; simple but amazing; full of consolation; worthy of our earnest heed. Come, Holy Spirit, and help us to discover for ourselves the wealth of meaning contained in these two words![13]

Jesus is "touched with the feeling of our infirmities" (Heb. 4:15 KJV), and it is a comfort to know that he knows. God knows all things, and he knows our tears and our darkness. But he knows

---

13 Charles Spurgeon, "Jesus Wept," sermon preached June 23, 1889, and published in *The Metropolitan Tabernacle Pulpit*, vol. 35 (Edinburgh: Banner of Truth, 1988), 338.

them not merely in the way that God knows all things—rather, in Christ he knows it through personal experience too.

Like Heman, we may feel abandoned and bereft, but believers are never alone. God stands with us in the darkness and grips us with his grace, even when we do not feel the grip of his hand.

Calvary enables us to lament, knowing that we do not do so alone. Christ feels our sorrows and weeps with those who weep. In the darkness, we have a friend who is closer than a brother (Prov. 18:24):

> For we do not have a high priest who is unable to empathize with our weaknesses, but we have one who has been tempted in every way, just as we are—yet he did not sin. (Heb. 4:15)

When we lament, we are never alone. We may not feel Jesus' touch, but he is closer than we could ever imagine. He laments with us and promises that one day the darkest night will end and eternal light will dawn on our souls. So for now we persevere, knowing that the God of peace gives us abundant peace, living hope, and amazing grace until the day breaks and the shadows flee away.

And there will be no lamenting in heaven.

Questions

1. "There is a line of teaching which insists that Christians should never suffer or experience pain of any sort. God wants you to be healthy, wealthy, and happy." Why is this

unhelpful? How do we know for sure it is wrong?

2. Read Psalm 39, which is closest to Psalm 88 in atmosphere and emphasis. What do we learn about the psalmist's circumstances here and how he responded?

3. The psalmist's experience of suffering "tempered him and made him stronger." How does this work? Is it always true that suffering makes us stronger? How do we make sure that we do not waste our pain?

4. How are the words "Jesus wept" full of consolation for you and for others whom you may be comforting?

5. The cross is the end of the story. Christ rose again and destroyed the fear of death (Heb. 2:14). How does this help us today when we lament?

8

Learning to
Hope

When Abe was born, he had a shock of blond hair. His sisters called him "the golden prince." But within a very short time, we came to realize that there was something seriously wrong with our precious little grandson.

After dreadful days of waiting, he was diagnosed with a rare neurological condition with a Latin name. That name can be translated as "smooth brain," meaning that Abe's brain had not developed in the womb, so he would not go on to develop the higher functions. He would never walk or talk or feed himself. In fact, he had less capacity for action than a newborn baby. And on top of that, this little Welsh boy had a limited life expectancy.

Edrie and I have experienced many waves of grief during our marriage—several miscarriages early on, the death of our parents and of Edrie's sister, and thirty years of struggling with the malevolence of multiple sclerosis. But holding Abe in our arms and mourning the wasted potential of this gorgeous little boy, witnessing the frequent epileptic episodes which wracked his body, watching the pain in the faces of his parents: these have been the deepest tragedies of our lives.

People have been wonderful. Many in our church grieved with us and wrote letters which overflowed with kindness. Friends assured us of their love and prayers. We received emails from people we had never met and letters that brimmed with compassion. We realized again just how wonderful it was to be surrounded by people who love you at such a time as this.

People have been wonderful—but they have not always been wise.

Shortly after Abe's diagnosis we were due to attend a Christian conference. I had no teaching responsibilities, so we easily could have ducked out. But we felt that it would be good to spend some time among friends, so we went. And they did not let us down. We felt loved and supported throughout.

But when we got home, I found an email waiting in my inbox. It came from an old acquaintance who had heard about Abe. After a few platitudes, this person wrote,

I'm so sorry. That must be so tough for your daughter. I suppose that the good thing is that he probably won't live very long.

Now, I am sure that this person was sincere and motivated by genuine compassion. But it was not what we needed to hear. In such a situation, it is probably better to say nothing, although it may be embarrassing to do so.

There is a real lesson in sensitivity here.

People need people

There is an old song which says that if you need people, you are lucky. I disagree. Needing people does not make you lucky—it makes you human! Human beings are created for relationships—first with God and then with each other. When God says that it is not good for the man to be alone, he is not just speaking about marriage—he is making a statement about human nature (Gen. 2:18). We cannot flourish in isolation.

We need each other. This is true generally, but it is particularly true when we face grief. Lamenting is often personal and private. However, when we lament, we also need people to lament with.

Secular society recognises that one of the strongest aids to recovery is social support. Relationships are vital to healing, and the burden of grief will be lighter when shared. The Bible recognizes the importance of this, demonstrating it within the church—God's new humanity:

Rejoice with those who rejoice; mourn with those who mourn. (Rom. 12:15)

Carry each other's burdens, and in this way you will fulfill the law of Christ. (Gal. 6:2)

And let us consider how we may spur one another on toward love and good deeds, not giving up meeting together, as some are in the habit of doing, but encouraging one another—and all the more as you see the Day approaching. (Heb. 10:24–25)

Support of grieving people can take many forms—words of comfort, assurances of love, or gestures of practical care. It is important that we don't walk away from grieving people just because we find their situation embarrassing or we are lost for words. And when we grieve, we should be willing to receive the help which is offered. It is tempting to put up a wall. But instead, we should enjoy the friends that God gives us and realize that the God of compassion is ministering to us through them.

Over the years I have been asked how to behave towards those who are grieving. Here is some of the best advice that I have gleaned from books on grief counselling and from my own personal and pastoral experience.

DO:
- Weep with the one who weeps
- Give spiritual support
- Pray for God's comfort
- Give emotional support and urge them to exercise self-care
- Encourage talking, and learn to be a good listener
- Acknowledge any achievements or milestones in recovery
- Give tangible physical or material support
- Always respect the confidentiality of what people share with you
- Maintain a healthy detachment throughout

DON'T:
- Diminish the vileness of death

- Speak judgementally
- Belittle in any way the suffering of the bereaved
- Imagine "one size fits all" when it comes to dealing with grief
- Use platitudes—e.g., that time is a great healer
- Compare your experiences, unless there is a very fitting comparison (and even then, tread lightly)
- Forget to take good care of yourself

Most importantly, be honest and be human, and speak the truth in love. Recognize that Christians grieve too, and grieve deeply, and that tears are God's gift to us:

Tears are proper for believers—indeed they should be all the more copious, for Christians are more sensitively aware of every emotion, whether of joy or sorrow, than those who have known nothing of the softening and enlivening grace of God.[1]

Lament shows solidarity with those who are suffering. We love our neighbours when we allow their experience of pain to become the substance of our prayerful compassion. People are sometimes disillusioned with the church because it can be triumphalist and give the impression that there is no room for pain and sorrow. When lament is expressed in our corporate worship

1   J. Alec Motyer, *The Message of Philippians* (Downers Grove, IL: InterVarsity Press, 1984), 90.

and our sermons, we are showing people that their pain matters.

But what do we actually say? As we should know by now, there is a way of using a theological argument that does more harm than good. It is not the fault of the argument itself, but of the one using it. Like medicine, real truths can be applied incorrectly. Think of Job's comforters. Their words contain hefty theological truth, but applied in such a way that it crushes Job. At the end of the book, God rebukes the comforters because they have not spoken the truth about him as Job has done (Job 42:7–9).

Study the words of Jesus. He always spoke the truth—even when it was painful—but his words did not crush people (Matt. 12:15–21). He is a perfect example for us to follow. When people grieve, they need compassion, truth, and hope.

What if … ?

It can be hard enough to bring comfort when the loss is that of a believer. But what if the person who died was not a believer? We want to say something that is both helpful and true. We want to provide comfort, but we cannot lie. What should we say?

First, we must not speculate. We cannot give false hope, but neither should we speculate unhelpfully about the person's ultimate destiny. We don't have infallible knowledge of the state of someone's soul before God. There may have been clear evidence right at the end of a life that the person was not a believer, but in my experience, this is rare. The story of the thief on the cross teaches us that it is possible to cry out for mercy on the brink of eternity. The thief's faith was real, and one day we will meet him in heaven. My mum cried out for mercy when we thought that she was on her deathbed. Amazingly, she recovered and in the last years of her life became a faithful disciple of Jesus.

Secondly, we can trust God to do what is right. When God revealed to Abraham his impending judgement on Sodom and Gomorrah, Abraham responded with a question:

Far be it from you to do such a thing—to kill the righteous with the wicked, treating the righteous and the wicked alike. Far be it from you! Will not the Judge of all the earth do right? (Gen. 18:25)

The answer to the question is that of course God will. Deciding on the fate of any individual is above our pay grade. We need to be honest about the reality of hell and the fact that salvation is through faith in Christ alone, but without surrendering these truths, we have to leave people in God's hands. God will do right by the person who died. This may not be the outcome we may have wished for—after all, God did judge Sodom. However, we can be certain that the final outcome will be just and right. We can rest in what we already know of God's character, and this is where our focus lies.

Thirdly, we need to remember heaven. When we arrive, God will wipe all tears from our eyes (Rev. 21:4). Sorrow and mourning will flee away forever. In the shadow of the cross, Jesus reminded his disciples,

Now is your time of grief, but I will see you again and you will rejoice, and no one will take away your joy. (John 16:22)

Speculating about the destiny of our loved one is futile. Assuming that he or she is lost, and torturing ourselves thinking about that person's pain, is a harmful and fruitless exercise. We must leave our friend or family member with God and remember that one day God's everlasting comfort will remove all our sorrows.

In the meantime, God has promised to give us the grace we need to deal with our loss. He will enable us to find comfort and strength in him. This will, in turn, enable us to support others in their grief:

Praise be to the God and Father of our Lord Jesus Christ, the Father of compassion and the God of all comfort, who comforts us in all our troubles, so that we can comfort those in any trouble with the comfort we ourselves receive from God. (2 Cor. 1:3–4)

This is not easy—but it is honest.

Encourage one another

We don't need to be in doubt when we think about what medicine we need to apply to grieving souls. Paul addresses this very question in 1 Thessalonians 4:13–18.

Paul had planted the church in Thessalonica during his second missionary journey (Acts 17:1–9). He had been forced to leave because of persecution, and although he had wanted to return, he had not been able to do so (1 Thess. 2:17–18). So he sent Timothy instead (1 Thess. 3:1–3). When Timothy returned to Paul, he reported on the condition of the church (v. 6), and one of the issues he raised was the fate of those believers who had died before Christ's return. Reading between the lines, it seems that there was confusion among these Christians. Paul had taught them to get ready for the second coming, and they were eagerly looking forward to it. But some of their number had died. This led to an anguished cry: "If only they had stayed alive until Jesus returned, we would be together with him. Does their death mean that they have lost their hope of heaven?"

Maybe it was even more personal than that: "What about my dad? He trusted Jesus before he died. Will I ever see him again?

It is to answer such questions that Paul writes this section of the letter.

Note how he begins and ends the section:

Brothers and sisters, we do not want you to be uninformed about those who sleep in death, so that you do not grieve like the rest of mankind, who have no hope. … Therefore encourage one another with these words. (vv. 14, 18)

Paul begins by recognising the reality of grief in the experience of genuine believers. As we know, grief can tear our life to shreds. Christians are not immune, and we must learn to be honest. But we are not without hope, "like the rest of mankind."

Because of the dual realities of grief and hope, Paul ends by calling for the Christians in Thessalonica to encourage each other with the truth, an expression of their love and mutual support which he has spoken of throughout the letter:

> Now about your love for one another we do not need to write to you, for you yourselves have been taught by God to love each other. And in fact, you do love all of God's family throughout Macedonia. Yet we urge you, brothers and sisters, to do so more and more … ." (4:9–10)

> Therefore encourage one another and build each other up, just as in fact you are doing. (5:11)

> And we urge you, brothers and sisters, warn those who are idle and disruptive, encourage the disheartened, help the weak, be patient with everyone. (5:14)

With these words

As a demonstration of this love, they are to comfort each other with "these words"—that is, the words in 1 Thessalonians 4:14–17:

> For we believe that Jesus died and rose again, and so we believe that God will bring with Jesus those who have fallen asleep in him. According to the Lord's word, we tell you that we who are still alive, who are left until the coming of the Lord, will certainly not precede those who have fallen asleep. For the Lord himself will come down from heaven, with a loud command, with the voice of the archangel and with the trumpet call of God, and the dead in Christ will rise first. After that, we

who are still alive and are left will be caught up together with them in the clouds to meet the Lord in the air. And so we will be with the Lord forever.

In these words, Paul is outlining four great truths.

Truth 1: A gentle sleep

Notice first how Paul describes the death of a Christian believer. Three times in three verses (4:13–15) he refers to them as having "fallen asleep": "those who sleep in death" (v. 13); "those who have fallen asleep in [Jesus]" (v. 14); and "those who have fallen asleep" (v. 15).

This is a common biblical picture of death (see Gen. 49:33; Acts 7:60; 1 Cor. 15:20). But we need to be careful here. The Bible does not teach "soul-sleep." Death is the separation of the body and the soul. Solomon writes of this in poetic terms in Ecclesiastes:

> Remember him—before the silver cord is severed,
>   and the golden bowl is broken;
> before the pitcher is shattered at the spring,
>   and the wheel broken at the well,
> and the dust returns to the ground it came from,
>   and the spirit returns to God who gave it. (12:6–7)

For the believer, it is only the body that sleeps—the soul enjoys the bliss of Christ's immediate presence. Paul longed for the experience that lay the other side of death:

For to me, to live is Christ and to die is gain. If I am to go on living in the body, this will mean fruitful labor for me. Yet what shall I choose? I do not know! I am torn between the two: I desire to depart and be with Christ, which is better by far … (Phil. 1:21–23)

Jesus' body rested in the grave, but his soul returned to be with his Father in a bliss which he shared with the repentant thief (Luke 23:38–46).[2]

The metaphor of sleep is comforting. We associate it with rest and refreshment. The battles of life take their toll on our frail bodies. But after death, the conflict is over, and the body finds rest, while the soul rejoices in its contemplation of Christ. But the other thing about sleep is that it is temporary. All things being equal, we expect to wake up! And that is what Paul describes next.

But before we move on, can you see the way this truth can be used to comfort those struggling with grief? When Mr. Blackman lost his wife, they had been married for over sixty years. The pain was excruciating. But through his tears he told me,

Lily isn't lost. I know exactly where she is. She is with Jesus, and Jesus is with me, and one day we will be together again, and we will never part.

"Comfort one another with these words."

2   I believe that Revelation 7:14–17 may describe this state: disembodied but glorious.

Truth 2: A great awakening

For the Christian, the experience between death and the return of Christ is blissful, as we rest from all pain and sin and contemplate the beauty of Christ. But it is not the final state. There is life after death, but there is also life after life after death! The latter is an embodied life, after Christ raises us in immortal bodies.

Paul tells us what he has received "according to the Lord's word" (1 Thess. 4:15). He did not invent this, and it is not the result of either logical enquiry or careful observation. But God revealed it to him. Paul may be referring to the words of Jesus when Jesus was predicting his own return:

Then will appear the sign of the Son of Man in heaven. And then all the peoples of the earth will mourn when they see the Son of Man coming on the clouds of heaven, with power and great glory. And he will send his angels with a loud trumpet call, and they will gather his elect from the four winds, from one end of the heavens to the other. (Matt. 24:30–31)

Jesus really died and was really laid in the grave. After three days, his heart began to beat, his eyelids flickered, and breath filled his lungs. His body and soul were reunited. He rose from the grave in the same body that had died on the cross, but which was now totally transformed.

The resurrection is the foundational truth of the Christian gospel. It is not the result of some arcane philosophical speculation or an elaborate hoax. It is not a parable or a myth or an existential experience. It is an event in history which changes everything. In the words of C. S. Lewis:

Jesus has forced open a door that had been locked since the death of the first man. He has met, fought and beaten the King of Death. Everything is different because he has done so.[3]

Jesus' resurrection means that he is now alive and will one day return in glory and majesty. This is the dominant theme in 1 Thessalonians, mentioned in every chapter of the book (1:9–10; 2:19–20; 3:13; 4:13–18; 5:1–11). It is the motivation for passionate evangelism and fervent discipleship. It is also a cause of great joy and comfort:

One word of command, one shout from the archangel, one blast from the trumpet of God and the Lord himself will come down from Heaven! Those who have died in Christ will be the first to rise. (4:16 Phillips)

It is the Lord himself who returns—the same Jesus who ascended to heaven (Acts 1:9–11). The "word of command" suggests authority and urgency. The shout of the archangel reminds us that Christ returns at the head of the armies of heaven (Rev. 19:11–16). The trumpet is used to summon people, and on

3   C. S. Lewis, *Miracles: A Preliminary Study*, rev. ed. (New York: HarperCollins, 2015), 237.

this occasion to wake the dead from the slumber of death (1 Cor. 15:52).

Those whom we have lost to death are not lost to us. Their souls, currently with Christ, will be reunited with their transformed resurrection bodies—bodies which will resemble the resurrection body of Christ. He has become the firstfruits of the resurrection of all his people (1 Cor. 15:20–23). He is the seal guaranteeing their bodily resurrection. He is also the model which demonstrates the nature of this new body.

So do not fear that those who have died before the return of Christ have missed out in any way at all! They will live again in gloriously new bodies. Elsewhere Paul describes it in these terms:

> The body that is sown is perishable, it is raised imperishable; it is sown in dishonor, it is raised in glory; it is sown in weakness, it is raised in power; it is sown a natural body, it is raised a spiritual body. (1 Cor. 15:42–43)

"Comfort one another with these words."

Truth 3: A glad reunion

But there is more.

> Those who have died in Christ will be the first to rise, and then we who are still living on the earth will be swept up with them into the clouds to meet the Lord in the air. (4:17 Phillips)

The word "swept up" or "caught up" refers to a sudden and powerful action. It means to seize and forcibly remove. This is usually referred to as the "rapture." Perhaps we should think of it in terms of the way in which God removed Elijah from earth to heaven (2 Kings 2:11–12).

Christians disagree about the timing and nature of the event—whole churches have been ruptured by disputes about the rapture! But surely the principal thing to grasp here is that it is not a matter for speculation but for anticipation. For those who grieve over the lost loved one, the message is clear: you will see them again. They will rise first. Then we rise. Then we are together *forever*.

Heaven is not a place of solitary contemplation—gazing at God and unaware of the presence of anyone else. It is a place of many mansions (John 14:1–4), and we will join a number which no human has the capacity to count (Rev. 7:9).

Will we know each other? I think so. Earlier in this letter, Paul told the Thessalonians that he loved them and wanted to visit them, but the devil blocked his way. However, even if he does not see their faces here on earth, he expects to see them and rejoice with them when Christ returns:

For what is our hope, our joy, or the crown in which we will glory in the presence of our Lord Jesus when he comes? Is it not you? Indeed, you are our glory and joy. (1 Thess. 2:19–20)

The clear implication is that when he meets them on that day, he will know them. On earth, Jesus loved to reunite grieving people with those they had lost.[4] When he returns, he will do this on a truly grand scale!

I miss my dad. He has been dead for nearly four decades now, but I often find myself longing to share things with him. Grief is more like a dull ache than a raw emotion. But I know that I will see him again, and part of the joy of heaven will to be catching up with him.

For the believer, death is never a final parting.

"Comfort one another with these words."

Truth 4: A glorious consummation

The final great truth is the capstone to everything that has gone before: "And so we will be with the Lord forever" (4:17).

We ache to be reunited with those we have lost. We yearn for our new bodies, in which there will be no trace of pain or sorrow or weakness. We long for the time when there will be no sin and evil in the world and in our hearts—when Christ will reign in perfect righteousness.

We pine for that place where lamentation ends forever.

But none of these longings comprises the heart and essence of heaven. The final goal of all God's people is "to glorify God and enjoy him forever," as the Westminster Catechism says. It is the presence of God which causes heaven to be heaven:

No longer will there be any curse. The throne of God and

---

4   Matt. 9:18–26; Luke 7:11–18; John 11:17–44.

of the Lamb will be in the city, and his servants will serve him. (Rev. 22:3)

At the very heart of this service will be the contemplation and enjoyment of God: "They will see his face, and his name will be on their foreheads" (Rev. 22:4).

God is our goal, and the service of God our occupation. And we do not need to choose between these sublime blessings. Pastor and author Ray Ortlund puts it like this:

How big is your hope? Is the wingspan of your hope big enough to get you soaring? Is your hope big enough, imaginative enough, with wolves and lambs and lions thrown in for good measure? Hope on this grand scale—this is the gospel. It is big. It offers both the prospect of personal intimacy with God forever and a renewed world of peace and righteousness. It isn't just one or the other. God has a plan for you and for this whole world. The Lord Jesus Christ died for this, and he will not be denied.[5]

Our Abraham recently celebrated his fifth birthday. This precious little Welsh boy has brought tremendous and unexpected joy to our family. I am convinced that when my wife and I begin to explore heaven in our new resurrection bodies, we will meet a striking young man in a brand-new resurrection body. He will

---

5   Raymond C. Ortlund, Jr., *Isaiah: God Saves Sinners*, Preaching the Word (Wheaton, IL: Crossway, 2005), 445.

greet us, and we will know immediately that he is Abe. Because he will speak in a Welsh accent!

And together, we will enjoy serving and contemplating our God forever.

"Comfort one another with these words."

Questions

1. Read Hebrews 10:24–25. Who is responsible for pastoral care within the church? And how does the writer to the Hebrews describe the kind of care we should give?

2. Look at the advice about how to treat people who are grieving. What does this look like in practice?

3. How is death like sleep? How is it not like sleep? What comfort does this bring us?

4. Read 1 Peter 1:3–5. How does Peter describe the nature and security of Christian hope? How could we use this passage to comfort those who are grieving?

5. One of the most difficult challenges we face is sensitively trying to help someone grieve for an unbelieving friend or relative. What might you say in this situation?

EPILOGUE

I sat down to write this book on the morning of Thursday, September 8, 2022. During lunch, I switched on the television to catch the news. It was dominated by one story only:

> The Royal Family have cancelled their engagements and travelled quickly to Balmoral, where the Queen "remains comfortable" after her doctors said they were concerned for her health.

Pictures of a plane arriving in Scotland with members of the Queen's immediate family and reports from the gates of Balmoral continued throughout the afternoon.

My wife and I were in the car when the radio reported that Queen Elizabeth II had died. An historic moment. I felt myself tearing up. I don't cry very often, and I could not explain my reaction. On the one hand, I felt a sense of deep sorrow. It was the passing of an era. Only the oldest among us had ever known another monarch. On the other hand, there was a sense of thankfulness—pledges had been kept, and a faithful servant was returning home to her Master.

The next few days were marked by profound national lamentation. People stood in queues for hours, often overnight, to catch a glimpse of the queen's coffin and pay their respects. Even those with no royalist sympathies joined in the national mood. Amazingly, there were few, if any, discordant notes.

But why such profound lamenting? Surely, it is because that is the way God has made us.

Tears are natural.

And they are natural for Christians as well.

Jesus wept. Job wept. David wept. Jeremiah wept. Their weeping became a matter of public record. Their weeping, sanctioned by inclusion in our Holy Scriptures, is a continuing and reliable witness that weeping has an honoured place in the life of faith.[1]

We need to learn to take off our masks and be honest and authentic about our battles with sin, doubt, fear, pain, and loss.

We need to be honest with God and regularly talk with him about our struggles.

At the same time, we need to dwell on God's faithfulness and

---

1   Michael Card, *A Sacred Sorrow: Reaching Out to God in the Lost Language of Lament* (Colorado Springs, CO: NavPress, 2005), 11.

rest in his embrace.

If we preach or teach from God's Word, we need to include lamentation among the topics we address.[2]

We need to model lamentation in prayer.

We need to be careful when selecting songs for worship, ensuring that we avoid theological triumphalism.

We need to allow room for lamentation in our regular worship service.

We need to weep with those who weep, offering them compassion, truth, and hope.

Above all, we need to learn to lament.

2   See Walter C. Kaiser, *Preaching and Teaching from the Old Testament* (Grand Rapids: Baker Academic, 2003), 121–134.

GIVEAWAY

RECEIVE FREE
RESOURCES EVERY
MONTH WHEN YOU
SUBSCRIBE TO
UNION PUBLISHING.

UP

SCRIPTURE INDEX

OLD TESTAMENT

Genesis

2:17	28
2:18	161
2:24	21
3:5	132
3:8	108
3:22	132
18:25	165
49:33	169
50:20	32

Exodus

1:15–22	64
3:7	152
15:24	16
16:1–3	64
16:2	16
16:7–9	16
17:3	16
20:1–17	138
34:6–7	54, 88

Numbers

11:1–6	16
11:11–15	48–49
20:1–3	16
20:1-13	64

Deuteronomy

29:29	91
32:4	88

1 Samuel

17:4	96
18:7	95
16:12-13	108
21:10–15	96

2 Samuel

11–12	121, 138
11:27	122
12:13	131
12:9–10	134
12:13–14	122
18:33	25

1 Kings

4:31	139
19:10	49
21	59

2 Kings

2:11–12	174
25	50

1 Chronicles

25:1	139

Job

1:1	34
1:8	34
1:20–22	33, 66
2:3	34
3:3	34
3:11	34
3:20–22	34
5:7	43
6:2–4	87
14:1	43
38–41	91
42	91
42:1–6	58–59
42:5	109
42:7–9	164

Psalms

3	66
4	66
5	66
6	123
7	66
9	66
9:7–8	69
10	66
10:1	69
10:2	70
10:4	70
10:5	70
10:7–9	70
10:10–11	71
10:12	71
10:15	71–72
10:16–18	72
12	66
13	66
13:1–2	60
14	66
17	66
18:2	135
18:30	92
19:7–9	104
22	66
22:1	17
25	66
26	66
27	66
27:4	80, 136
27:8	111
27:13–14	111
28	66
28:7	135
30:5	32
31	66
31:9–12	63
32	123
32:1–2	126
32:3–4	122
34:1–4	97
34:8	88
34:18	26, 136
36	66
38	123
38:9–10	62
39	66
40:12–17	66
41	66
42	66
42:3–4	104
42:10–11	104
43	66
51	123
51:1–2	123, 133
51:3	123, 134
51:4	131
51:5	123
51:7	124, 133
51:8	124, 136
51:9	124, 133
51:10	125
51:11	136
51:11–12	124
51:12	136
51:13	125, 137
51:14	124
51:15	125
51:16–17	124